QUICKBOOKS ONLINE FOR BEGINNERS 2023

The Ultimate Guide for Small Business Owners to Mastering Quickbooks and Speed Up Your Bookkeeping

Thomas Worley

Table of Contents

INTRODUCTION 5

CHAPTER 1: QUICKBOOKS ONLINE 7

  Types of QuickBooks Online 9
  The Desktop Versions of QuickBooks Pro and Xero 12

CHAPTER 2: KEY STEPS TO GETTING STARTED WITH QUICKBOOKS ONLINE 15

  The Simple Steps to Set Up a Complete Working System 16
  The Features of QuickBooks Online 17
  Difference of QuickBooks Online from Desktop 18

CHAPTER 3: THE ADVANTAGES OF QUICKBOOKS ONLINE 20

  QuickBooks Online Simple Start 21
  QuickBooks Online Essentials 21
  QuickBooks Online Plus 22
  Other QuickBooks Online Advantages 22
  Why Is QuickBooks Popular? 31

CHAPTER 4: INVOICING AND STATEMENT CREATING 32

CHAPTER 5: PAYROLL AND EMPLOYEE'S PAYMENT HISTORY 37

  How to Add Employees 38
  How to Process A Pay Run 38
  How to Create Timesheets, Leave, and Expenses for Employees .. 39
  Creating Expenses for Employees 40
  How Employees Can Self Service 40
  Setting Work Zone App for Employees 41
  Enabling Work Zone 42

CHAPTER 6: HOW TO PLAN CASH FLOW, PROFITS AND REVENUE WITH QUICKBOOKS + 11 METHODS TO OPTIMIZE REVENUE AND INCREASE PROFITS 44

- Accounts payable 45
- Deposits 45
- Retained earnings 46
- Building a cash flow projection chart 46
- Ways to Optimize Revenue and Increase Profits Using QuickBooks 47

CHAPTER 7: PAYING VENDORS 49

- Switch on the Purchase Order Option 50
- Generate and Email Purchase Orders 50
- Amend Purchase Order Statuses and Include Them on Bills 51
- Choose the Plan That Suits Your Business 53
- Let QuickBooks Handle Invoicing Requirements 53
- Offer Various Payment Solutions 53

CHAPTER 8: BOOKKEEPING AND QUICKBOOKS 55

- How Does QuickBooks Live Bookkeeping Work? 57

CHAPTER 9: INSIGHTS AND REPORTS 60

- Overview Of Reports And How To Customize 61
- Summary Reports 65
- Detailed Reports 66
- List Reports 67
- Transaction Reports 67
- Creating And Saving Customized Reports 68
- Comparative Reports 69

CONCLUSION 73

GLOSSARY 75

Introduction

With an online accounting software such as QuickBooks Online, you don't need to be on-site all the time to keep track of your accounts. This is especially useful for growing businesses. The small monthly fee makes this software affordable for just about anyone.

QuickBooks Online has many features, including an expense tracker that allows you to track expenses by category. It also has a general ledger, which helps you keep track of transactions and reports. The software also lets you scan receipts, which saves you time and helps you maximize your tax savings.

Subscription service

Subscription service for QuickBooks online is a great way to stay up to date on your business's financial information. The program uses the same security protocols as top banks to protect your information. It also encrypts backup tapes and files. You can also sign up for additional features like online training or business analytics. The basic subscription will cost you $49 per month. But, there are higher-end subscriptions available for larger businesses. While most people still consider subscriptions as cloud-based services, this is not the case with QuickBooks. Intuit offers a standalone application, QuickBooks Desktop, for businesses. You can also sign up as an authorized reseller for QuickBooks, which allows you to sell the software directly to your clients. Authorized resellers are knowledgeable in the QuickBooks ecosystem and offer complete business solutions.

Easy to use

Easy to use QuickBooks online is an accounting program that allows you to customize your business's features, from importing your company's data to automating processes. It can also help you automate the creation of recurring invoices and bill payments. In addition, it automatically backs up data to the cloud. It can reduce fraud risk as well. This software has an AI program that audits 100% of your spend reports, which makes it easy to protect your business from fraudulent transactions.

It eliminates the need for spreadsheets and enables businesses to get paid quickly. It also allows businesses to customize invoices and track business trips.

Cost

When you're ready to start using QuickBooks online to manage your finances, you'll need to decide how much it will cost. You can choose a single-user license for $25 per month or a multi-user license for $180 per month. Each option offers different benefits. If you're running payroll twice a month, the cost will be $88 per employee per month.

Features

QuickBooks Online offers a variety of features that can make managing your finances much easier. It can track invoices and payments, print checks, and import your financial transactions from your bank account. It also allows you to set up custom user roles and can protect your data by creating backups and restoring previous versions. Moreover, it can manage your payroll and track your employees' time. In addition, QuickBooks Online has several integrations with popular business applications, including Salesforce, HubSpot, and DocuSign.

Chapter 1:
QuickBooks Online

QuickBooks online is a cloud-based service that Intuit offers. It is known as QBO for short. The user pays a monthly fee for subscriptions rather than the user paying upfront for this particular service. This monthly fee allows the user to gain exclusive access to this software using a web browser and a secure and private logon. Intuits makes available upgrades regularly and patches for the software regularly, just that it includes pop-ups inside the apps that are due to added paid services.

Difference between QuickBooks and QuickBooks Online

QuickBooks Online is a subscription-based service and includes more advanced inventory accounting. Both programs offer desktop apps. In addition, each version supports multiple users.

The biggest difference between Desktop and QuickBooks Online lies in their platform. Desktop is hosted on a computer, while QuickBooks Online is cloud-based and accessible from anywhere. Desktop is not cloud-based, and is only available for use with a computer that has the correct version and software. Desktop users typically own several versions of QuickBooks software.

It has a subscription-based pricing model

Intuit offers a free trial period for QuickBooks users, and you can also receive a special deal for the first three months. After the trial period ends, you can choose from a variety of plans. For example, the self-employed plan costs $15 per month and is designed for freelancers and sole proprietors.

There are three main plans offered by QuickBooks Online. Basic, Plus, and Advanced. Each plan includes a specific number of users and access to the software. The basic plan allows three users, but the Advanced plan is designed for five or more users.

Intuit has been focusing on QuickBooks Online for a long time, and has done so by bringing the software up to feature parity with the desktop version. In fact, many in the Quickbooks community expect the desktop version to go away in the near future and be replaced by the online version. As a result, the company's website focuses heavily on its online version.

It has more advanced inventory accounting

This popular accounting software provides many features that can make inventory management easier for small businesses. QuickBooks Enterprise has more advanced inventory management features than the free version, but you'll have to spend more money to use it. For a more affordable option, consider using QuickBooks Premier Plus, which has similar inventory management features.

One feature of QuickBooks Online that makes it easier to manage inventory is multichannel tracking. This feature allows you to track inventory in multiple channels, including online, in stores, and in a warehouse. You won't find this feature in QuickBooks Desktop, so you'll need to invest in QuickBooks Commerce.

It offers multi-currency functionality, inventory tracking, auto-updates of quantities, and tax integration. In addition to these features, QuickBooks Online is compatible with Boxstorm Pro, which provides advanced inventory management capabilities. It also supports lot/batch number tracking, expiration date tracking, and customer management.

Types of QuickBooks Online

When it comes to choosing a software program, the options are almost endless. There are basic programs, the Basic Start, QuickBooks Self Employed, QuickBooks Pro, and QuickBooks Premier, to name a few. For larger businesses, you'll want to opt for the Plus version, which offers tracking features for Locations and Classes. It also allows you to track larger jobs, including purchase orders. Franchises also often opt for the Plus version, which has an inventory feature.

QuickBooks Self Employed

You can call QuickBooks's support center for help, or you can use the community forum. Both methods offer plenty of support for questions and issues, and the knowledge base is well-organized.

QuickBooks Pro

A comprehensive accounting software, QuickBooks is a powerful solution for small and midsized businesses. With an easy-to-use interface and customizable accounting features, it is easy to use and master. Users can easily set up and manage business accounts, track business expenses, manage customers, vendors, and employees, and even create professional invoices.

QuickBooks Premier

Its features include industry-specific reporting. It offers 150 sales reports, 150 financial tax reports, and the ability to customize industry reports. However, it does not support subsidiary and parent reporting. Moreover, it does not feature bin location tracking.

Besides, it is not compatible with bar code capabilities unless an add-on feature is purchased.

QuickBooks Enterprise

Whether you're new to QuickBooks or looking for a way to streamline your business' accounting, the online version of QuickBooks can help you succeed. This software has a number of advantages over QuickBooks Desktop, including a simplified learning curve, access on multiple devices, and an array of automations and applications. However, QuickBooks Enterprise has some limitations. For instance, it lacks some industry-specific capabilities and customization capabilities. Furthermore, you must renew your license annually. And, unlike QuickBooks Online, you won't get ongoing support.

QuickBooks Mac Plus

QuickBooks Mac Plus offers a host of useful features and functions for small businesses. Among these are the tools needed to maximize tax deductions and manage cash flow. In addition, it can create professional-looking invoices and accept payments.

Disadvantages of QuickBooks Online

Some of the disadvantages of QuickBooks Online include its limited support for backups and restoration points. If you need to handle a large volume of transactions, the performance of the program can suffer. Additionally, it cannot be used from mobile devices. If you need to manage your finances in the field, you may wish to consider other options.

QuickBooks Online's performance suffers when you need to handle large transaction volume

While you may be able to manipulate data with ease, the performance of QuickBooks Online will be affected if you are handling a high volume of transactions. This is because the software was built for small businesses and its file size is limited. As your business grows, so will your transaction volume.

If you need to reconcile accounts on a large scale, you should back up your company file before starting the process. While it's not necessary, backing up your file before making any changes can help you avoid unnecessary performance degradation.

One way to improve the performance of your account is to make sure you enter all of your transactions in a sequential fashion. This way, your records will be accurate from the start date forward.

If you are unable to access QuickBooks online using your mobile device, you may be experiencing a security problem. If this is the case, you must update your device to a newer version of Chrome or create a new Intuit account with improved security.

You can access QuickBooks Online on a mobile device if you have a ProAdvisor membership. You can use QuickBooks Mobile on your mobile device to manage customers, record expenses, reconcile bank transactions, and view reports. The app also has a feature for jumping directly to the Chart of Accounts.

Desktop Versions of QuickBooks Self-Employed

If you run a small business, you may be wondering which version to choose. While QuickBooks Self-Employed has an online counterpart, it is much easier to use if you use a desktop version. It also has features that make it much easier to manage your business, including tax preparation and reporting. Taxes can be a huge burden for business owners. QuickBooks Self-Employed helps you reduce your tax burden by calculating your estimated tax obligation using your business' revenue, expenses and tax filing status.

QuickBooks Self-Employed

Desktop versions of QuickBooks Self-Emploied are designed specifically for small businesses. They can be used to track and categorize transactions in a business, and they can also be used to send tax payments to the IRS. These programs are particularly useful for small businesses because they can save both time and money. In addition to their tax-related functions, QuickBooks Self-Employed can help you manage your personal finances, keeping track of business expenses, and more.

Many of these products have free trials, so it's worthwhile to try one out. Also, don't forget to check out the system interface and navigation, as these features can be very important to you. Finally, consider the customer service and support for the program.

QuickBooks Online Plus

When choosing which desktop version to purchase, make sure you take your specific business needs into consideration. If you plan to handle heavy inventory and large projects, you should choose the Plus version. Essentials will cost you $30 less per month than Plus.

Both QuickBooks Self-Employed and QuickBooks Online Plus allow users to send and track invoices, keep expense receipts, and keep track of mileage. Both have easy-to-use interfaces and include features that will streamline your bookkeeping and minimize your workday. QuickBooks Online is also compatible with a wide variety of apps.

QuickBooks Pro Plus

Intuit's QuickBooks Self-Employed offers an intuitive dashboard to track all of your business' expenses and income. You can filter your data using the search bar or by choosing from a variety of sorting options. The app even allows you to manage your deductions and sales taxes.

The setup process for QuickBooks Self-Employed is straightforward and easy. Next, you'll see a new tool called the Tax Timeline, which can guide you through the steps required to set up TurboTax. You'll be asked to input basic information about your business, tax situation, vehicle, and healthcare. You'll also need to enter login information for online bank accounts.

The Desktop Versions of QuickBooks Pro and Xero

If you're in the market for a new accounting software, you can't go wrong with QuickBooks Pro. Its powerful features are designed for businesses that want more. These include advanced product tracking by style and employee commission tracking. Plus, QuickBooks Pro also offers the ability to manage up to 20 stores from one office. All desktop and online QuickBooks products are compatible with merchant services accounts, which handle credit card payments, bank transfers, and debit card transactions. This direct payment integration eliminates a lot of work and error.

Quickbooks Pro

If you are running a small business, you need to make sure that you have the proper software for your needs. First, it can be used for payroll. You can set up payroll for employees and manage the expenses of your business. Next, you can connect your bank accounts and pay bills with ease. It also makes bank reconciliation easy since most entries are automatically posted.

Lastly, the desktop version offers additional navigation options. It has a menu bar with drop-down capability that provides you with easy access to system features. The menu bar also offers additional features like My Shortcuts and Run Favorite Reports.

QuickBooks Enterprise Diamond

The new QuickBooks Enterprise Diamond desktop version adds more features and protection for sensitive data. With a monthly subscription, you can track job costs and change orders, manage inventory, and compare profit and loss statements. It also comes with a new interface, more than 200 apps, and a new security feature that allows you to assign security to specific employees.

This desktop version also includes a subscription to the Premier Plus or Pro Plus versions, a mobile device with an Internet connection, and a QuickBooks account. You'll need the same version of Microsoft Office as the desktop version. This includes Office 2013 or 2019 (32-bit or 64-bit). You'll also need the same version of Intuit Statement Writer software.

Xero Desktop

There are many benefits to using Xero for your business. In addition to managing all your accounting needs, Xero offers an intuitive interface that lets you send estimates and invoices quickly and easily. It also offers time tracking capabilities for invoices and can pull up data on contact details, inventory and pricing. You don't have to login to the web to use it, and it has a cloud-based interface that makes it more convenient. Additionally, Xero is more affordable than other accounting software options. Unlike many competitors, Xero doesn't charge late fees. Moreover, you don't have to install any additional software to use it.

Desktop Versions of QuickBooks Advanced

The desktop versions of QuickBooks Advanced can be installed automatically or manually. Once installed, the software will create a shortcut on your desktop. To open it, you'll need to enter a user ID and password. You can then choose to automatically open the program or manually start it. You can even download and install a demo version if you want to try it out first.

QuickBooks Silver Edition

The Silver Edition is the most economical version of the software available. It supports the basic functions of QuickBooks, as well as customer support, product upgrades, and advanced reporting. For those with more extensive accounting needs, you can consider the QuickBooks Enterprise Gold edition.

QuickBooks Desktop Enterprise

Deleted sales orders can now be deleted in batch from QuickBooks Desktop Enterprise. Instead of deleting each one, the software will record these transactions as unapplied customer credits in the Accounts Receivable account. Moreover, QuickBooks will allow you to view inventory stock status by item and its valuation summary.

This accounting software is suitable for small and medium-sized businesses and can be configured for anywhere from one to 30 users. It includes features like inventory tracking, advanced reporting and pricing, and file-sharing capabilities.

QuickBooks Premier

QuickBooks Online Advanced is a powerful program for small businesses, but there are some differences between it and the desktop versions. The desktop version costs an annual fee, while the online version is free. QuickBooks Online is more flexible and convenient to use, since it's hosted in the cloud.

QuickBooks Online Advanced

QuickBooks Advanced is designed for larger companies and comes with special features and services. QuickBooks Advanced supports 25 billable users and three accounting firms. It also offers batch invoice generation and batch upload of up to 1000 transaction lines. It supports 48 unique active custom fields. Some features require a third-party subscription.

In addition to QuickBooks Online, there are various desktop versions of the software for your small business requirements. There are three predominant tiers, including Mac Plus, Desktop Pro Plus, and Desktop Premier Plus.

Chapter 2:
Key Steps to Getting Started With QuickBooks Online

Overview

If you are a small business owner, you may want to take a look at the QuickBooks Online program. This program has many powerful features that can make your job easier. It can be used to send invoices, track sales, and run payroll. It also offers an audit trail that shows you exactly who logged into the program and who logged out.

To use QuickBooks Online, you'll need a software-as-a-service (SAAS) license. This program is compatible with desktop and mobile devices, and it lets you access data from anywhere. In addition, SAAS is a way to use the software without having to hire an IT staff to run the software.

If you are running a small to midsize business, QuickBooks Online is one of the best options. You can also attach files, such as invoices, to transactions. The program also includes a feature to track billable hours. This feature categorizes them as employee or client hours and lets you add them to an invoice. This feature is useful for service and hourly businesses that need to track employee and client time.

The Simple Steps to Set Up a Complete Working System

When you set up a working system, you should consider the goals of each user and their role in the overall process.

Goals of each user in a working system

Identifying the goals of each user is crucial to the successful design of any product or system. These goals are not always explicitly stated by the user, but they can be inferred by analyzing the data. The design team should try to understand these goals in order to come up with a solution that will fulfill these goals. This way, the team can ensure that the product or system is going to add value and be used by people. In order to identify these goals, the designer must be able to empathize with the user, and determine what their needs are.

In a working system, the goals of each user can be translated into monetary values. Every time a user completes a goal, the amount is recorded in a report.

Work-intensive and time-consuming phase

The process of setting up a complete working system involves a series of phases. The first is known as the integration phase, and this involves the process of connecting and integrating separate systems. This process requires precision and can take time. However, if successful, it can automate several business processes and provide accurate data. After the integration phase, the system must undergo operational testing to ensure that it is error-free.

Budgeting is a process whereby you estimate how much money you expect to spend over a period of time. It can be used by an individual, group of people, business, or government organization.

The first step in setting up a budget is to determine how much money you can afford to spend each month. Make sure you include money set aside for saving or debt repayment. If you find that you have been overspending in a certain category, you can adjust the budget accordingly. Using a budgeting system can help you avoid unnecessary debt and make it easier to make wise financial decisions.

Planning

The planning phase starts with an initial analysis to determine the project's objectives and problem.

The Features of QuickBooks Online

This means that they don't have to install traditional software on their computers and don't need to worry about operating system compatibility. The program is available on any Internet-connected computer, which makes it very convenient for businesses.

QuickBooks Online is a popular accounting solution for small businesses

QuickBooks offers more advanced options for small businesses. It lets you view customized sales and profitability reports and track data by office location, department, or job phase. In addition, you can track time and expenses by category.

It offers a variety of features

QuickBooks Online offers features for managing your unpaid bills and expenses. It offers advanced invoicing options, including the ability to create recurring payments. In addition, you can create recurring transactions, record partial payments on invoices, and send payment reminders.

It has a convenient remote access option

QuickBooks Online has a convenient remote access option for users to use the service from a remote location. To use this option, the user of the remote computer must have a web browser and be logged in to the QuickBooks account. The user can then select remote screen share options, such as automatically lowering the screen resolution, setting the remote computer to a full-screen mode by default, and disabling the keyboard and mouse. The user can also access their account and all files on the remote computer. Remote access requires a higher monthly payment than the standard option.

Another convenient feature of QuickBooks Online is its ability to make recurring transactions. This feature allows you to set up recurring bills, checks, deposits, and invoices.

Difference of QuickBooks Online from Desktop

If you're considering switching to QuickBooks Online, you may be wondering what the difference is. Here are a few things to consider. First, cloud-based accounting systems are often more user-friendly and have more automations. Desktop-based programs may not have all of the features of cloud-based applications, and you might be better off sticking with the desktop version.

QuickBooks Online is a desktop-based accounting system

If you are a small business owner and you're looking for an accounting system, QuickBooks Online is an excellent choice. The software is easy to use and has many benefits, including an AI-powered solution that streamlines expenses and bills processing. This program is also a great choice if you don't want to deal with multiple applications.

In addition to being a cloud-based service, QuickBooks Desktop is also available. It has many advantages, including an intuitive interface and a number of navigation options. In addition to inventory management, the desktop version also provides industry-specific features such as cost-of-labor-hours, inventory tracking, and barcode scanning.

It's easier to use

If you're thinking about moving from desktop to online accounting software, QuickBooks Online might be the perfect solution. The software can be used on any device with an internet connection, and you'll have access to your business's financial data from any location.

It has more automations

QuickBooks Online is a web-based version of the traditional accounting software that allows business owners to easily and efficiently manage their books. The cloud-based application syncs data in real-time, so users do not have to worry about manual data entry. However, QuickBooks Desktop has a steeper learning curve, and its interface is not as modern as QBO's.

It's cheaper

The monthly subscription plan for QuickBooks Online is cheaper than that for the desktop version. For example, a Premier plan has 150 customizable reports, while a Simple Start plan is for one user.

Chapter 3:
The Advantages of QuickBooks Online

Remote access is one of the chief reasons people love using QuickBooks Online's intuitive platform. It gives you, an accountant, or a bookkeeper, the ability to log in and view financial data from any web browser.

With your company's analytical information at your fingertips, it's now possible to operate a business worldwide. Customers can pay you in multiple currencies and immediately if need be. If you own a service business, QuickBooks Online can help you scale your enterprise to international levels.

Below are some benefits that QuickBooks Online offers organization owners:

- Accountants and employees have easier access to data.
- Based on the cloud—no high-end computer or constant updates required.
- Superior customer support.

- Utilize automatic downloads to sync your business information everyday.
- All data and backups are stored on Intuit servers.
- Automatically or manually, send statements and invoices.
- Download and send the report autonomously.
- ACH and credit card payments.
- Track VAT.
- Connect to your bank.

Maybe you've forgotten that QuickBooks Online comes in three different subscription levels. Let's go over the benefits these additional tiers offer:

QuickBooks Online Simple Start

Simple Start comes with 20+ built-in business reports and is available to one user. This package is perfect for any new small company and gives them the ability to manage their finances.

Here are the benefits of subscribing to the Simple Start tier from QuickBooks Online:

- Credit card and bank reporting tools.
- Send limitless invoices, statements, and estimates.
- Subscribe to the Payroll option to manage staff salaries.

Starting with this version of QuickBooks is a great way to get the feel of the application and see if it works for your business.

QuickBooks Online Essentials

You'll receive everything in the Simple Start plus more when you select this option.

With 40+ business report features and open to up to three users, the Essentials package provides you with more options. This tier allows you to send invoices in multiple currencies, manage employees, and gives you insights into the performance of your enterprise.

QuickBooks Online Plus

You get all the benefits included in the Simple Start and Essentials packages with extra additions. Managing budgets, tracking projects or locations, monitoring inventory, and generating recurring transactions are the inclusions in QuickBooks Plus. These subscriptions can be utilized by five users and the business accountant, giving you total control of your business.

Other QuickBooks Online Advantages

Without accurate business records, it'll be challenging to scale your company or get funding from a third party or bank. A business's financial health is the first thing investors and lenders want to know about before putting money into it.

If your books aren't up to date or you're disorganized about filing taxes, things could quickly become a nightmare. What company owner wants to land in trouble with the IRS? Luckily, QuickBooks Online takes care of all the hassle by making its platform user-friendly.

Intuitive User Interface

Most accounting applications come with little to no educational material, are challenging to learn, and have clunky user interfaces. The design and layout of QuickBooks Online not only make managing your cash simpler but more succinct, even if you have no experience in finance or accounting.

Integration With Third-Party Applications

QuickBooks Online has a massive list of applications and services it can connect to. Whether you are using a third-party tax preparation program or Microsoft Excel, QuickBooks Online makes it easy to connect.

There are over 650 business apps that the platform can integrate with, including:

- Shopify
- Adobe Commerce
- Amazon Marketplace
- Google Cloud Storage Buckets
- Cleo Jetsonic
- Oracle E-Business Suite
- Microsoft Dynamics
- Acumatica
- Netsuite
- Salesforce
- SAP

No matter what type of business you operate, I'm certain that QuickBooks Online can help take it to the next level.

Customization

Creating business plans, charts, spreadsheets, and invoices has never been easier. QuickBooks Online offers you a selection of practical templates, which can be customized to suit the business's requirements.

The customization options help make documents look professional and stand out from the competition. Company owners can add their logo, detailed information about the sale, or notes to inform employees or clients about something special.

Check Signing

The check signing process becomes efficient when you have the option of uploading your signature.. That is useful for people who sign many checks because it saves precious time and frees up availability. If you sign hundreds of checks each month, you'll love this!

Affordable Pricing

Most new companies have limited budgets to work with in the beginning stages of operation. Furthermore, if those proprietors spend an exuberant amount on accounting software, they'll be out of business in no time.

There's no need to hire an accountant to take care of your books externally, as it all happens in a single location. You can have more time and avoid paying an external vendor to maintain your transactional records.

If you have trouble learning QuickBooks Online, there's always an option to use the live bookkeeping service. A certified bookkeeper will determine your business's financial health and manage your books.

With a starting price of only $12.50 per month, QuickBooks Online is not only affordable but has robust features too.

Used by Millions Worldwide

QuickBooks Online is one of the most popular accounting software programs globally, and truthfully so. There are many finance firms, accountants, and bookkeepers who love using this software to manage business finances.

If you have never used accounting software before or are feeling lost in the system, a qualified individual can help you. Ensure you work with someone who has QuickBooks Online Certification for peace of mind.

Cloud Storage

Cloud Storage provides you access to your financial records no matter where on earth you are situated. If your accountant is in the United States and you're in Australia, the process of adding a bookkeeper to the subscription is simple.

Give these individuals access to your company file by providing them with the password and login details. Choose from a dynamic range of financial or accounting firms and get your books done correctly.

Your information is stored on Intuit's highly secure server, meaning if your computer malfunctions or is damaged, all data remains intact.

Money Management

Small to medium-sized organizations love utilizing QuickBooks Pro Online for their fund handling functions. One of the top attributes of the application allows business owners to set transaction details and due dates for all recurring invoices.

You can email, print, or message directly from the application, and all data is recorded for easy accessibility.

Let's not forget the fact that the platform can connect to your bank account and download transactions. This function removes the requirement for paper bank statements and allows you to view all fiscal data in QuickBooks Online's overview.

Expense Billing

All businesses have several costs and expenses that must be taken care of for the company to operate optimally. It could be larger fees, such as purchasing new machinery for the factory, or smaller charges for dinner or gas.

Irrelevant to the type of expense, QuickBooks gives you the ability to record each one. Moreover, expenditures are documented in correlation with the project or customer, giving you the option to search for them through the dashboard.

Sales Invoicing

Generating invoices and creating receipts are required for any company. With QuickBooks Online, you can now perform the most imperative business functions with a single click or with the shortcut keys.

Once the invoice is created, it can be sent electronically to clients via email or printed. Depending on the project, you can charge your customer in large batches or separately. The former is a valuable feature that allows you to charge multiple clients for the same product or service.

If you want the advantage of accepting credit cards and debit card interests, signing up for QuickBooks Merchant Services should be your go-to.

Financial Reports

There are many financial reports users of QuickBooks Online can generate. Whether it's weekly, monthly, or yearly, QuickBooks gives you the option to consolidate data into one place. Furthermore, reports can be exported to Excel and delivered to your accountant via email. Below you'll find some of the most common financial reports you can view in QuickBooks Online:

- Trial Balance
- Statement of cash flows
- Transaction list with splits
- Recurring template list
- Transaction list by date
- Reconciliation reports
- Recent transactions
- Profit and Loss
- Recent automatic transactions
- Profit and Loss comparison
- Journal
- General ledger
- Balance sheet
- Account list
- Balance sheet comparison

These features are the tip of the iceberg when it comes to financial reporting, so make sure to utilize them to increase company effectiveness.

Job Costing

Track expenses, monitor time, and create estimates on projects you are currently busy on. This helps you determine job profitability and run detailed cost reports to locate areas of interest.

Without accurate estimations, your business may fail to land that client you have been wanting.

Customer Support

The customer support users receive from QuickBooks Online is phenomenal. No matter what package you're on, the team at Intuit is ready and willing to assist with any issues. If there is a glitch with the software or you're stuck with the accounting, speak to the folks at the QuickBooks Online support center.

You can contact QuickBooks Online client services via email, live chat, or phone. As long as your organization has a paid subscription, you can access the support service an unlimited number of times.

Training and Education

Resources like this book are the first steps to getting ahead with your QuickBooks Online education.

If you sign up for QuickBooks Online Enterprise, you'll receive online training tools at no cost.

Mobile Access

Service and subscription-based businesses benefit significantly from this feature as their clients are generally based worldwide.

Download the application to your smartphone and link it to your QuickBooks Online account to get started.

Focused on Small Businesses

QuickBooks Online loves helping small businesses take care of their accounting requirements. The application's budget-friendly prices and intuitive, user-friendly interface make it the perfect solution for anyone needing to maintain their financial records.

If your company is growing and you need more from the software, it is a matter of a few clicks and QuickBooks Online is upgraded. Speak to a consultant if you are unsure of the package that'll suit your company's requirements.

Tax Compliance

With payroll reporting and tax regulations, it can be challenging to keep track of all business transactions. QuickBooks Online monitors tax laws so that its clients don't have to. Thanks to the sales tracking features, QuickBooks can report business expenses and sales tax when the need arises. Moreover, it gives you the benefit of avoiding inconsistencies or miscalculations when sending in tax return documents.

Here are the advantages of automating the accounting process in preparation for tax season:

- Improve financial record accuracy.

- Reduces bookkeeping activities like calculating expenses and income.

- Automatic report generation for analytics, tax purposes, or financial statements.

- Eliminates the need to track down crucial information as everything is stored in a single location.

Additionally, the software helps you sort and categorize expenses, so all the data is available when you need it. QuickBooks Online gives you the ability to upload receipts or documents that are automatically segmented.

More Efficient Business Processes

When the financial management process is streamlined with an automated accounting system like QuickBooks, you can free up time for more imperative tasks. Tasks, such as categorizing expenses can be automated to limit mistakes or subsequent issues in your business's accounting.

Both old and new company owners struggle with monetary management tasks because they can be arduous. State-of-the-art software like QuickBooks allows enterprise proprietors with no experience to acquiesce to federal laws and control their accounting operations.

Better Client Relationship Management

Enabling direct payments and invoicing clients gives them a more fluid experience, allowing them to pay your business quickly by utilizing one of their favorite forms of remittance.

This reduces the hassles that typically arise when clients don't pay or are avoiding your invoices. Any business owner wants to keep the peace with their customers, and QuickBooks can help them do it. Improve your organization's cash flow management by having more consistent payments throughout the year.

With the extra free time you'll receive using QuickBooks, you can provide superior client services that can help grow your business exponentially.

Premium Security

QuickBooks Online is cloud-based and was developed to keep your sensitive company credentials secure. There is a double layer of security that protects all data transferred between you and Intuit's server.

The software utilizes a 128-bit SSL encryption to encode data and keep it safe at all times. Furthermore, your information is autonomously saved in case of system failures or a broken internet connection.

Your essential data is also backed up so it can be restored should there be an error. Safety is of the utmost importance to Intuit, and QuickBooks Online is a testament to that statement.

Accurate Forecasting

Making educated predictions to grow your business is done by understanding common trends within your enterprise. Scaling growth, planning for seasonality, and keeping your organization financially solvent can only be achieved through precise forecasting.

Raw data is turned into easily digestible analytical reports that help you plan for the future. With these insights, you can make more intelligent decisions concerning your enterprise's finances, such as cutting costs, allocating resources, or adjusting staff salaries.

Increased Productivity

With QuickBooks Online's accounting automation, various duties can be handled concisely. There'll be less time spent correcting records, inserting data, and clicking through files to retrieve reports.

Moreover, the attributes that require focus, such as approving transactions, documenting costs, and analyzing cash flow, are accelerated.

With all the free time on your hands, focusing on growing your company should be your number one priority.

Regular Updates

Intuit constantly releases updates to iron out bugs, increase security, and add additional features. Each upgrade comes with documentation that explains the fundamental changes incurred.

Irrespective of whether you subscribe to the Simple Start, Essentials, Plus, or Desktop version of QuickBooks, you can rest assured the software always operates optimally.

QuickBooks Is Expanding

By the end of the decade, QuickBooks is planning to reach over ten million users. The propensity for growth is a sure sign that the enterprise knows what's up. Customer orientation has always been at the forefront of QuickBooks' business model, and it shines through in the applications it creates.

QuickBooks Is Feature Rich

You already know by now that QuickBooks is loaded with features. Although it may take time to learn each aspect of the application, it'll all be worth it in the end. QuickBooks is on its way to becoming the most widely used accounting software with all these attributes.

Every business process is taken care of through the system; you only have to set it up. If you need to add additional features or options, it's a matter of upgrading your subscription.

Inventory Tracking

Knowing when stock is bought or sold can help you keep tabs on your business inventory. The system utilized by QuickBooks Online allows you to enter various data, including SKUs, stock codes, and other relevant information.

Succinctly track and manage any item your business uses to make money. *Please note*: Inventory tracking is only available to Plus users of QuickBooks Online.

Electronic Payments

Electronic payments make company processes simpler. Your patrons won't have to go to a financial institute to pay your invoices because of the wide range of credit cards accepted. All invoices have a link attached that the customer can use to pay debts immediately.

Also, transactions performed on your business account can be automatically downloaded and documented in QuickBooks Online.

Why Is QuickBooks Popular?

QuickBooks is doing what it has always done; that is assisting people with accounting software. Intuit sends surveys to determine user input and incorporates those suggestions into new updates.

Whether you own a large enterprise or are a solopreneur, the QuickBooks suite offers something for any executive. The dynamic range of features and reporting management capabilities make QuickBooks Enterprise sought after.

Now that you know everything there is to know about QuickBooks Online, it's time to speak to a consultant to find out how it can work for your business.

Chapter 4:
Invoicing and statement creating

An invoice is a document that provides a detailed description of the products and services you have provided to customers and their respective prices. If the customers do not pay you at the time of the sale, then you need to keep track of what they owe you to ensure that payment is made in the future, so invoices help you manage your account receivable. Invoices are therefore used for sales made on a credit or part payment.

If your business does not use the estimate feature, just start with "create invoices".

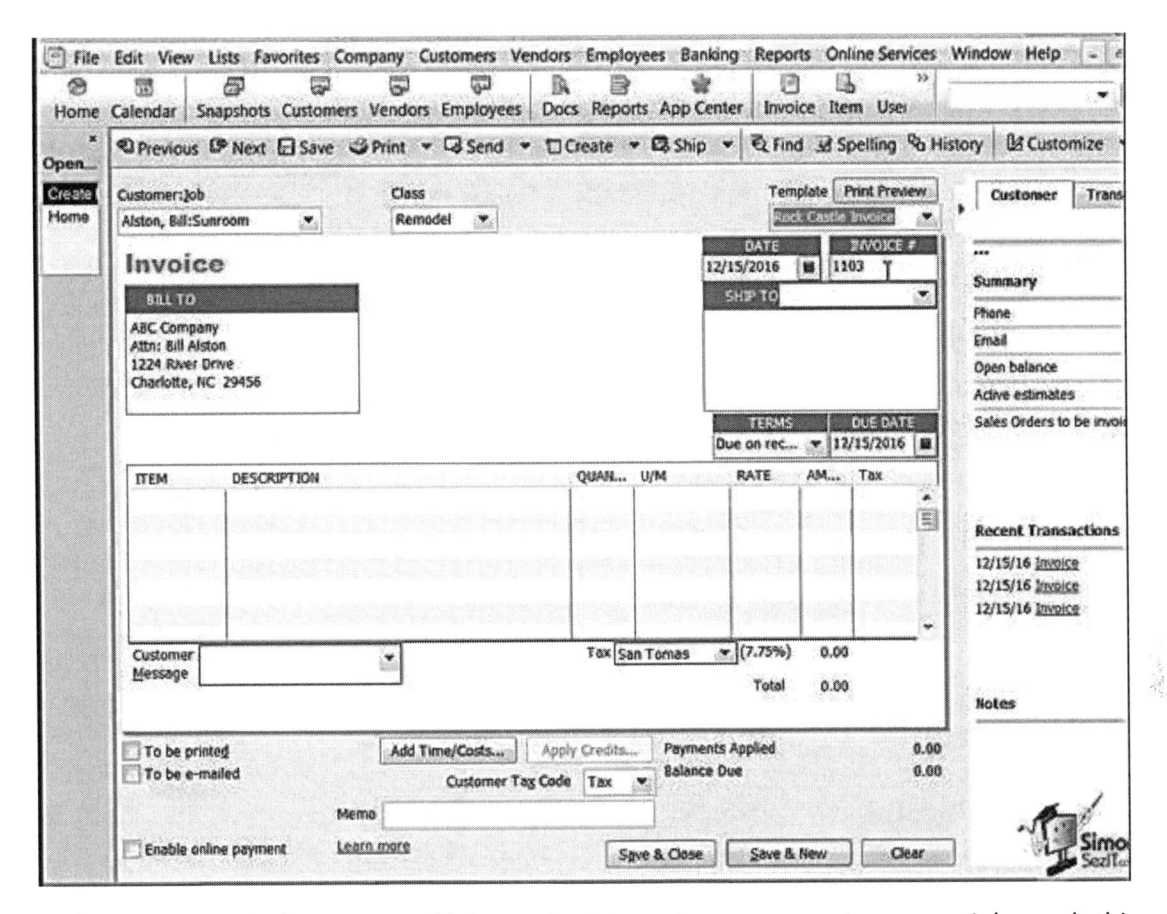

In the invoice window, you will be asked to enter your customer or job, and this information will appear based on how you set up your customer. Next, you will also be required to enter the class you would like to associate this invoice with. After that, you will find the template list. In QuickBooks, you will have several predefined templates for invoices. You do have the ability to customize these or create your own. You will also have to enter the due date for this invoice as other options, such as the invoice date, invoice number, and terms would have already been provided by QuickBooks based on your previous settings.

At the bottom of the invoice, you will be required to enter some details. Under "items", there's a drop-down arrow where you can see the list of available items. Other details to include here are description, quantity, unit of measurement, and tax, and you will also notice that QuickBooks would calculate the quantity times the rate to give you the amount.

33

Below your items, you will see your Customer message window. Here, you can include an appreciation note to your customers. To the right, you will see the sales tax rate that this particular customer is charged. So you will notice it tells you the actual rate and the amount of sales tax charged on the total invoice. Below this, you will see the total amount of the invoice itself.

Below the invoice on the right, you will see a couple of checkboxes, "to be printed" and "to be emailed". If you would like to print and email a batch of invoices, you could certainly do that and email or print them all at once.

Receiving Payments

After creating an invoice, you will want to get paid, and you can do this with QuickBooks. This is important because you need to ensure you are not working for free, and secondly, you need to reconcile your bank statements with QuickBooks.

To receive payments, you can go in two ways. You can use the desktop Icon that says "receive Payments," or you can go into the top menu that says "customers", click on it and select "receive payments".

Enter the details in the appropriate boxes. These include the customer you are receiving from, the payment amount, and the payment method. Make sure the date matches your bank statements, so you do not have issues when reconciling these transactions. When you enter all this information, you need to confirm that you have selected the correct invoice you are getting paid for and that the amount you receive is correct. If everything is entered correctly, you can complete your journal entry by clicking "save and close or save and new".

I suggest you check your accounts receivable reports weekly to keep track.

Invoice Simple makes the invoicing process easy

If you run your own small business, creating invoices can be a time-consuming task. Using an online invoicing software makes the process easier by making it simple to create, edit, and send invoices. It makes it easy to create and send invoices in multiple languages and formats, and supports a variety of payment methods. You can use this service to create customized invoices for clients, win more work, and build trust.

Invoice Simple also lets you track which invoices are due and which ones have already been sent out. This way, you'll know exactly how much income you've made and when it's time to send your invoices. You can also easily share your information with your accountant so that you can track your finances properly. The software saves your invoice items and client details, so you don't have to type them over again. You can also import phone contacts and use predictive typing, which means that you can create invoices without looking up information.

Steps in invoicing

When creating invoices, companies must follow several steps to process them. First, the invoice must be recorded in the company's accounting software. This includes verifying the amount billed and itemised goods. If there are discrepancies, the invoice must be corrected immediately. Next, the invoice is routed for approval. When all of the steps are completed properly, the invoice can be approved right away.

Once this is complete, invoices should be sent out. The best way to do this is through email. Make sure to use an uneditable PDF file and make sure the subject line includes your business's name and address. You can also include your invoice details in the body. This can help you get paid faster. Another way to ensure you get paid on time is to call your customers to confirm receipt. If they have not paid, you can politely remind them that they are still due for their payment.

Rules for invoicing

When creating invoices and statements, there are a few general rules to follow. For example, you should not discuss individual purchases on the invoice - instead, your statement should include a list of totals. Invoices and statements are typically sent out at periodic intervals. Usually, businesses send them out at the end of each month or quarter. The purpose of these documents is purely informational, so it is important to keep that in mind.

When you are creating an invoice, you can also use a custom field to set up certain details. Usually, custom fields will be available for certain items, such as department telephone numbers. These fields can be used to customize invoices for a particular department. You can also add specific information to your customer statements.

Payment due date

When setting up an invoicing workflow, you will often want to specify a payment due date for each invoice. You can do this before the invoice is generated by setting up a Payment due date limit. This limit will be calculated based on when the invoice was delivered or when the customer received it. This limit can be configured on the Due date limits page in the Accounts payable or Accounts receivable tab.

The payment due date is one of the most important details when setting up an invoice. Having an accurate due date will make it easier for your customers to make payments, while a timely payment will make it easier for you to keep track of your invoices. In addition, if you're trying to collect late payments, a due date is very important for ensuring that you get paid on time.

Chapter 5:
Payroll and employee's payment history

Setting up employee payroll in QuickBooks is simple; employees can not only view and download their pay stubs, but they can also enter their information.

All that is required is to send them an email inviting them to log in and enter information about the activity they have completed or the workforce before they are set up in QuickBooks.

Below are the steps to recording and reporting taxes:

- Go to "Payroll", then click on "Employees".
- Select "Add Employee", and then input the employee's name.

- Check the section that enables workers to submit their personal information and access their payslips online using QuickBooks, and then enter the employee's email address.

On the invite employees page, click on "Invite Employees". The employees will get a link to QuickBooks Online Workforce to enter their personal information. This includes their name, gender, and birth date. They can also enter their address and work information.

QuickBooks will immediately add workers to the list of active employees after they have entered all the essential information, but the list will still display them as incomplete.

Add employment details such as payment schedule and payment history for every employee, tax information, and the workplace pension.

After you complete the form, click on "Save".

How to Add Employees

Gathering basic information on your workers, such as their name, date of birth, and current contact information, is necessary before you begin.

Employees can be found by selecting the "Employees Section" menu option.

If this is your first employee, add them to the list.

Input the employee's payday, method of payment, and amount paid.

You will be asked to fill out various forms in the following field based on your response to whether the employee has been paid since you started.

Select "Save and Continue."

How to Process A Pay Run

After you've set up payroll in QuickBooks and added employees, you're ready to create a pay run. A pay run only needs to be set once for the date part, after which all subsequent pay runs will be moved to the next pay date period.

Once you open the pay run screen, select "Pay Schedule". Input the date for the pay period ending and when the pay run is paid, then click "Create".

Following the click of the create button, the next screen displays a summary of all employees in that run, including tax and their salaries or earnings. By clicking on the individual employee, you can view more information about them.

The action button is important because it allows you to make additional selections to correct or amend the employee pay run.

After making all the necessary changes, employees' full details can be hidden by clicking back on the employee's name.

Look for any warnings before completing the pay run. Click on it to get started.

After filling in the information needed, click "Save" and note any prompt alerts for an action.

To finish the pay run, click on "Finalize Pay Run" and verify that the date paid is correct, then click "Finalize."

Payslips can be sent to employees quickly using the payslip option.

After it has been finalized, the pay run is now locked. Only before any bank statements are processed can they be unlocked and changed. Once the pay run is complete, download the files that will be uploaded to the bank, run any payroll reports, and send payslips.

How to Create Timesheets, Leave, and Expenses for Employees

Creating Employee's Timesheets

Employees who are required to use timesheets will be able to view, create, and delete timesheets on their own from within the Work Zone app.

Employees must use timesheets in the employee details, Pay Run defaults page, Payroll Settings, and Employee Portal Settings if they want to access timesheets in Work Zone.

Select the timesheet icon on the bottom of the screen.

Tap the timesheet area on the homepage.

Click on "Employees".

Click on the "Manage Employees" tab.

Select "Create a Timesheet".

Select the employee's name and select the week.

Select the "Work Time". Put the start time, end time, break taken, and their location/

Click "Save".

Click on "Manage Employees".

Select "Create Request" and choose the employee.

Select "Leave Category" and enter the period the employee will be on leave on the first and last days of the leave. The system will calculate and estimate the number of required leave days.

Click on "Approve Immediately".

Creating Expenses for Employees

Click on "Manage Employees".

Click on "Create Expense Request".

Select the employee and the description of the expense being paid for

Input the expense date, the category, and the location. You can add a note choosing the tax code and the amount of the expense.

You can click on approve immediately or leave it empty and click on the "Create" button.

Now your expense request will reflect on the next payroll.

How Employees Can Self Service

If an employer grants access to the portal, the employee will be instructed to activate their account and log in.

Follow these steps to activate your account:

To begin, open the email inbox associated with the email address that you provided to your employer.

Find and open the email with the subject line "Login Information for Your Company Payroll."

Return to your email inbox and locate the email with the subject line "User Account Created."

In this email, you will be provided with the username for your portal account. This is the username for which you have created a password.

Click the email link that directs to the employee dashboard, which will take you to the login page.

To access the self-service portal, log into the portal using the password and the username

Setting Work Zone App for Employees

Download work zone from google play store or iOS.

View login settings in the gear button.

View own personal payroll details on employees list.

View the business access.

Contents on the Home Screen

Any content which requires employee acknowledgment.

Leave balances.

The last payslips.

Timesheet.

Expense summary

Next shift time.

Contents on the Profile Icon

Employee details.

Bank account.

Payment summaries.

Super funds.

Leave.

Emergency contacts.

Other documents.

Enabling Work Zone

This feature is not enabled by default. You will enable it in the business portal so that employees can use it from their smartphones. You must navigate to "Payroll Settings" and then "Employee Portal Settings".

The sub-settings are optional, but they will affect the employee workflow when clocking in and out. The following settings must be used:

When employees clock in or out, take photos of them.

Allow employees to log in with a higher classification.

Allow employees to use scheduled start and finish times when clocking in and out.

Send reminder emails to employees.

Save.

Summary

Payroll administrators can review the detailed payment history of employees. They have the right to void or issue replacement payments if they find an error. This feature is available in most payroll systems. Using the payroll history reports can help payroll administrators avoid payroll errors. There are several types of payroll reports.

The Payroll Detail Report lets administrators view a summary of each employee's paycheck. They can sort the list by name, location, and department. They can also view the earnings of all workers over a specified period. They can also view the company's payment history. This report will show them the total amount earned, withholding taxes, and other costs.

Guide

This publication explains your responsibilities as an employer in relation to taxes and employee payment history. It describes withholding, reporting, paying, and depositing, as well as the forms that you must provide to employees and send to the IRS or SSA. Throughout the publication, the terms "income tax" and "payroll tax" refer to the federal income tax.

Chapter 6:
How to plan cash flow, profits and revenue with QuickBooks + 11 methods to optimize revenue and increase profits

In order to plan your cash flow, you must know how much money you'll need to spend. To do this, you can use QuickBooks. The software has tools that help you keep track of income and expenses. The important thing to remember is to keep the balance between assets and liabilities. As you plan your cash flow, make sure that Assets = Liabilities + Owner's Equity, or AE/OE. You must also add your contributed capital to your assets.

Accounts payable

QuickBooks has a feature called the Cash Flow Projector that allows you to see your projected cash flow for any given period. It also has a separate report that shows your expected business expenses and payments for the specified period. By matching up the time periods of an expense and payment report, you can easily see your cash flow and see where you can make changes to improve your cash flow.

When you are creating a cash flow forecast, the most important step is to have accurate financial data. Using QuickBooks's Cash Flow Forecast tool, you can see how your cash flow will change over the next six weeks. This information can help you tweak your business strategies so that you can maximize your cash flow. QuickBooks's Cash Flow Projector feature can also help you stay on top of your expenses and make sure your employees get paid on time.

A cash flow forecast is a crucial component of your cash flow plan. It helps you determine your cash needs and predict incoming revenue. This forecast is usually based on the short and long-term outlook. You can use QuickBooks' Cash Flow Forecast to determine how much cash you need to run your business and plan accordingly. If you're not sure how to set up a cash flow forecast, don't worry, there's an expert QuickBooks support team available to help.

Deposits

To plan your cash flow, you must first know where your money is going. This is an essential step to avoid short-term cash crunches. QuickBooks can help you plan your cash flow by allowing you to view your accounts receivable and other income sources at any given time. For instance, it can show you which invoices are coming up and which ones are past-due. It will also allow you to follow up on late payments.

Once you've identified what's going into each bank account, you can use the Cash Flow Projector feature in QuickBooks. This is a relatively simple tool that helps you forecast your cash flow. It is especially useful for short-term forecasts. It shows you how much cash you have coming in and going out for the next six weeks. This can help you make sure you're able to pay employees on time.

You can also use QuickBooks Online to create a cash flow statement and run an accounts receivable aging report. The Statement of Cash Flows can also be customized. You can filter it by employee, vendor, and product to see detailed numbers for each account. The Balance Sheet, meanwhile, shows the balance between your company's debts and assets.

Retained earnings

QuickBooks has a feature that can help you plan cash flow. The Cash Flow Projector is a simple tool that allows you to look at your accounts payable and expenses and estimate the amount you will receive and spend over a specified period. You can also use Excel to match up time periods so that you can see your cash flow.

Cash flow forecasting can help you maintain the financial stability of your business. By determining what you will need to pay employees and suppliers, you can plan your cash flow accordingly. If you have a small business, you can also use Cash Flow Forecast to determine your projected revenue for the upcoming period. However, this feature is only available in QuickBooks Desktop editions and not QuickBooks Online.

You can create reports to help you improve cash flow. For example, you can use the Sales by Product or Service report to determine the most profitable products and services. This report shows total sales for each product or service, and it also shows the sale transactions for that product.

Building a cash flow projection chart

Using a cash flow projection chart can help you avoid a cash crunch. It can also help you take advantage of discounts. In some cases, bankers and investors require that you make a projection before they loan you money. It helps them understand how well you can manage your business and builds your credibility.

The first step in building a cash flow projection chart with QuickBooks is to identify your business' cash flow situation. Typically, the first column will be your operating cash, which is the amount of unused earnings in the previous month. The next column will show your projected accounts receivables and payables. You can calculate the expected cash you'll need each month by subtracting the estimated amount of each from your current cash balance.

Once you've figured out the cash flow projection chart for your business, you'll want to set the date range for the report. By default, QuickBooks will create a report for week-to-week cash flow, but you can change this to whatever interval you choose. This way, you can compare your projections to previous cash flows.

Ways to Optimize Revenue and Increase Profits Using QuickBooks

Using QuickBooks for your small business can be a huge asset, as the program can help you manage your cash flow. It also helps you reduce the time it takes to get paid. Days Payable Outstanding (DPO) refers to the average number of days it takes to pay your own invoices, and reducing this number will help you better manage your cash flow.

Segment your business by product or service lines

There are a variety of ways to segment your business by product or service lines using QuickBooks. Whether you sell products online or in stores, QuickBooks helps you manage your accounts in an organized and easy-to-understand manner. For example, you can set a credit limit for your customers and QuickBooks will alert you when an order exceeds this limit. This can help you decide whether to reject an order or ship products COD.

QuickBooks offers an inbuilt feature called class tracking, which allows you to categorize transactions. This feature can be particularly useful for local restaurant chains, which can track profit margins by menu item. It also allows you to create robust internal financial reports that can help you determine the profitability of each location. To enable class tracking in QuickBooks, navigate to the Account Preferences tab, click on "Details" and select "Class Tracking." Next, create a new class.

Automate bank and credit card downloads

Once you have connected to your bank account, QuickBooks will automatically download the maximum number of transactions available to you from that account. Most banks only allow you to download 90 days worth of historical transactions. If you need to download more than 90 days, you can configure the date range of the download in QuickBooks.

Once you have set up a system to download your bank and credit card transactions into QuickBooks, you can quickly and easily reconcile them. This will allow you to better gauge your cash flow situation and make more informed spending decisions. This will also allow you to better forecast your future cash flow.

Customize sales reports

Quickbooks Sales Reports are a powerful tool that provide a high-level overview of your sales. Whether you're a manufacturer or wholesale distributor, the reports can help you understand customer behavior and revenue to improve your sales strategy. You can also get granular details about transactions with the Detail Report, which summarizes sales by product or customer.

A key metric for growing companies is margin percentage. You may have to dig deep to find it. Luckily, it's available under the "Compare another period" option. Using this tool, you can quickly see how much revenue covers direct, indirect, and fixed costs. You can then make data-driven strategic decisions based on this information.

Track cash flow

Using QuickBooks's Cash Flow Report, you can analyze and improve your cash flow. The report shows how your business is performing over a specific period. It also provides historical information that helps you understand what factors affect your profits and losses. Knowing the numbers can help you make decisions about your business operations. You can also use the Cash Flow Projector feature to make short-term forecasts. The feature can predict your cash flow in the next six weeks and help you make sure you can pay your employees on time.

One of the best ways to improve your cash flow is to offer your customers the option to pay online. QuickBooks Payments, previously known as Intuit Merchant Services, allows you to accept payments online from an emailed invoice. Just like other merchant services, this feature integrates with QuickBooks so you can record the sale, credit card fee, and cash deposit automatically.

Chapter 7:
Paying vendors

QuickBooks Online makes it easy to create purchase orders and send them to vendors or suppliers. Luckily, the entire cycle is managed through QuickBooks' unique set of tools.

Easily generate purchase orders (PO) and email them straight to vendors when you need to order more stock. Without a purchase order, how will your vendors know you want to purchase more products?

Enter the specific quantity of the items you want to buy and send them to the dealer. Once they agree to the terms and accept the purchase order, the PO can be added as a bill or expense. This feature keeps your accounts stable and all monetary matters connected.

Switch on the Purchase Order Option

Follow these steps to turn on the purchase order feature if it isn't already on:

Head to 'Settings'

Click "Account and Settings"

Open the 'Expenses' tab

Navigate to the "Purchase Order" field and click 'Edit'

Switch on the "Use Purchase Orders" feature

Enter a standard message plus three custom fields if you feel inclined.

Once you're complete, click 'Save' and then 'Done'

Please Note: It's impossible to customize purchase order formats because QuickBooks sets a standard default layout for this feature.

Generate and Email Purchase Orders

Click '*+New*'

Open 'Purchase Order'

Choose a retailer from the 'Vendor' dropdown menu

Confirm their mailing address is correct.

If you're sending the items directly to a client, choose 'Ship' via in the 'Ship' dropdown.

Type in the "Purchase Order" date

Open 'Settings' on the "Purchase Order" form

Click "Choose What You Use" tab and select "Custom Fields for Orders"

Select 'Save' and send from the dropdown to email the PO to the vendor

If you want to send the purchase order in the future, it can be stored on the QuickBooks Online server by clicking "Save and Close." When you're ready to send the buyer's requisitions, head to 'Expenses,' locate the order, and click 'Send' in the 'Action' tab.

Amend Purchase Order Statuses and Include Them on Bills

The status of Purchase Orders is 'Open' once they have been created. To make the transaction official, you can add it to a bill or expense once the vendor accepts it. QuickBooks Online will convert the status to 'Closed' if you follow these steps:

Switching on Bill Itemization

Your bills must be set up to showcase the items in the 'items' section so you can circumstantiate services and products.

Head to 'Settings'

Choose "Account and Settings"

Click on 'Expenses'

Open "Bills and Expenses," and click 'Edit'

Select 'Done'

Include a Purchase Order on a Check, Bill, or Expense

Click on '+New'

Choose 'Bills,' 'Check,' or 'Expense'

Select a 'Vendor' from the 'Payee' dropdown menu on the purchase order form.

Click 'Add' to include new items on the specific order.

Tick the 'Billable' checkbox if your client is billed for a particular item.

Once complete, "Save and Close"

Add a Partial Purchase Order to a Check, Bill, or Expense

If you make a partial payment or have only received half of a purchase order, you can add that information to an Expense or Bill. That allows you to interconnect many transactions into a single purchase order:

Click on '*+New*'

Select 'Bill,' 'Check,' or 'Expense'

Choose a 'Vendor' from the 'Payee' dropdown menu.

Locate the correct purchase order and click 'Add.'

Change the amount or quantity to show what you have paid or received.

Click "Save and Close"

Viewing Your Open Purchase Orders

Select 'Reports' in the "Business Overview" tab.

Use the "Open Purchase Order List, Purchases by Vendor Details, Purchase by Product/Service Details, or Open Purchase Order Details Report" options.

Making Vendor Payments With QuickBooks Online Bill Pay

QuickBooks Online allows you to pay your vendors directly from the platform with a few clicks.

On the "Business Overview" dashboard, click on the "Bill Pay" widget

Open the "Make a Payment" tab

Enter all relevant payment information for the retailer, including:

- Class
- Customer
- Description
- Account
- Payment account
- Bill No.
- Memo
- Amount
- Vendor name

Click on "Choose Delivery Method"

If you are making a check payment, edit vendor data if required, and choose a processing date.

The Benefits of QuickBooks Vendor Payments

Not every company owner utilizes QuickBooks features to their full potential. This section provides you with an explanation of why you should be using QuickBooks Online Vendor Payments for your clients, consumers, and suppliers.

Choose the Plan That Suits Your Business

QuickBooks Online gives you the option to choose the plan that works best for your company. Customers have two options to select, which include a pay-as-you-go scheme for small business owners. With no monthly fees or obligations, it's the ideal solution for someone who wants to try out QuickBooks Online's payment processing services.

Business owners who use QuickBooks Pro, Premier, or Online often get charged 1.75% on transactions. With the exceptional savings you can experience on both packages, you can pass down better deals to your customers.

Let QuickBooks Handle Invoicing Requirements

We all know that time is money, and rightfully so. With QuickBooks Bill Pay, you have the benefit of getting more hours to focus on your company. Once you activate this add-on, it autonomously makes all monetary accounts congruous.

Customer books and invoices are automatically updated when changes are made. If you have a client who purchases the same service every 30 days, QuickBooks records this data and lets you generate recurring payments. This feature lets your patrons pay their invoices faster and frees up more time.

Offer Various Payment Solutions

When your consumers have multiple payment options, it benefits you and the purchasers. QuickBooks Online offers your clients two options for payment processing.

First, the customer can select the bank transfer-only option if they want to send cash directly to their business account. Secondly, the person can pay for your products or services via credit card or a standard bank transfer. Check payments are typically processed within three days and are a great way to increase overall sales.

Complete Transactions at Anytime

QuickBooks Online lets your customers pay via their computer's browser or on a mobile device. The easier you make payment for your clients, the more effective the entire sales process becomes.

Allows Clients to Feel Secure About the Transaction

Purchasing products online often scares clients because of hackers or cyber criminals performing unscrupulous acts. Fraud and identity theft are the primary reasons people are afraid to buy anything online.

Luckily, QuickBooks Online has high technology banking grade protection for both sides of the payment gateway.

Superior Customer Support

QuickBooks Online has tons of features and options to learn. Sometimes, this can be an issue for some users, but luckily, the company has an exceptional customer service department.

Whether you want to contact the support staff via phone, email, or live chat, they are responsive and willing to help at a moment's notice. There are also multiple video tutorials on YouTube and other websites that can help you master the program.

Other sources, like this book you're reading, are a great way to get to know the in-and-out of this accounting application.

There are a multitude of advantages your business receives, including those in the QuickBooks payment process. You'll never have to worry about invoices going unpaid because of the ease of use and the option to pay from anywhere.

Chapter 8:
Bookkeeping and QuickBooks

Bookkeeping and Quickbooks are two software programs for accounting. These two programs are similar but have some differences. Both offer many of the same features. There are also differences in their cost and requirements. This article focuses on QuickBooks. Read on to learn more. Quickbooks is the preferred software for small businesses and bookkeeping professionals.

Similarities

While there are many similarities between bookkeeping and Quickbooks, the two are not the same. An accountant's job description is more complex and requires a higher level of education, while a bookkeeper's duties are largely clerical. In addition, an accountant must be a CPA or have QuickBooks-related certification, while a bookkeeper doesn't need a degree.

Sage, which is also widely used in accounting, is similar to QuickBooks in a number of ways. Both provide robust inventory and accounting functionality. Sage also offers greater customization options. However, QuickBooks has a more user-friendly interface and is easier to learn.

Differences

QuickBooks provides tools to manage taxes and finances for business owners. However, users must ensure that the data they input is accurate and complete. Accounting professionals have specialized training and can perform account reconciliations that QuickBooks cannot do. This can lead to errors and mismatches in the records. Accountants also provide more comprehensive advice and support to business owners.

QuickBooks is not the only option for small businesses. There are other systems available, such as NetSuite. NetSuite has many benefits over QuickBooks, such as revenue recognition automation, which enables accounting teams to schedule revenue to be recognized automatically. It also allows businesses to generate accurate forecasts and financial statements. It's especially helpful for software companies that have multiple deliverables and need to have their financials accurate.

Costs

When it comes to bookkeeping, there are many options available for businesses, including QuickBooks or bookkeeping software. Whether your business is small and self-employed, or large and multi-location, QuickBooks can help you manage your finances effectively. In addition, it helps you reduce audit risks and puts your reports right at your fingertips. You can also take advantage of a number of subscription options for QuickBooks to suit your needs.

The cost of QuickBooks Live is typically lower than the cost of hiring an independent bookkeeper. With QuickBooks Live, you can interact one-on-one with your bookkeeper, who will perform both on-going and daily bookkeeping tasks. The service is also cheaper than hiring an independent bookkeeper who charges by the hour or per month.

Requirements

When choosing a bookkeeping program, it is important to choose the software that is best suited for your company's specific needs. Intuit QuickBooks has many features and functions that can help you manage your business's finances. Its multidimensional reporting system can eliminate the need for a complicated chart of accounts, and lets you track details at the transaction level. While QuickBooks tries to make this work by using tags, many users end up resorting to workarounds.

NetSuite, for example, has a built-in approval workflow that enforces segregation of duties and controls user access to certain data. It also supports multiple users and works well in a work-from-home environment. It can automate tasks such as exception processing and discount calculation, limiting the risk of errors due to manual data entry. It also offers powerful reporting tools and allows you to customize and manage user permissions based on company size.

How Does QuickBooks Live Bookkeeping Work?

Both new and established businesses have access to QuickBooks Live Bookkeeping. First, you'll need to schedule a one-time consultation with a real bookkeeper to determine your book line.

If you are a new business owner, these qualified bookkeepers provide instructions on setting up QuickBooks. You'll be given guides on how to link credit cards, add bank accounts, generate customized invoices, and establish a chart of accounts.

What Does QuickBooks Live Bookkeeping Cost?

QuickBooks Live Bookkeeping is sold at a monthly pricing tier and is obtainable by QuickBooks Online users. A cleanup fee of $500 is charged before beginning the process to ensure your accounting is up to scratch.

The pricing tiers work by calculating a business's average monthly expense over three subsequent months. After the initial month, your subscription amount is determined by the previous three months, except if you cancel.

Below is the current pricing structure available:

- $0–10,000 per monthly average - $200

- $10,001–50,000 per monthly average - $300
- $50,001–∞

Benefits of Live QuickBooks Bookkeeping

- Scalable pricing
- Tax-ready books
- Accurate books are guaranteed.
- A real-life accountant you can communicate with.

Drawbacks of QuickBooks Live Bookkeeping

- They won't handle your bill payments or send out client invoices.
- Your bookkeeper may fail to understand certain accounting concepts.
- They don't offer consultation services after you've signed up.

Alternatives to QuickBooks Live Bookkeeping

If you require bookkeeping features that help you run your business but don't have the money to fork out, you should seek out a QuickBooks alternative. There are a ton of applications for you to contemplate!

Whether you find your current QuickBooks monthly plans unsatisfactory or you want bookkeeping software for your new organization, checking out these alternatives is recommended:

- Buildium
- Sage 100 Contractor
- Sunrise
- Quicken
- Sage 50 cloud
- FreshBooks

Each one of these accounting applications does an excellent job of managing your company's books. A plus is that nearly all of them have a minuscule learning curve, so it won't take long to get your books in order.

Chapter 9:
Insights and Reports

QuickBooks Online has many customizable reports that can be extremely helpful in making business decisions. Customizable reports will summarize your data and provide reliable, up-to-date information that can be used in your day-to-day operations.

QuickBooks Online offers a wide range of reports depending on your purchased subscription level.

Overview Of Reports And How To Customize

There are several reports that you can run to understand your business better. You can find the reports from the *Dashboard* on the left-hand menu under *Reports*. Most business financials are comprised of three main reports: Balance Sheet, Income Statement (also known as Profit & Loss), and Cash Flow Statement, but QuickBooks Online provides many more statements that can be used for internal purposes.

Reports are divided into three tabs:

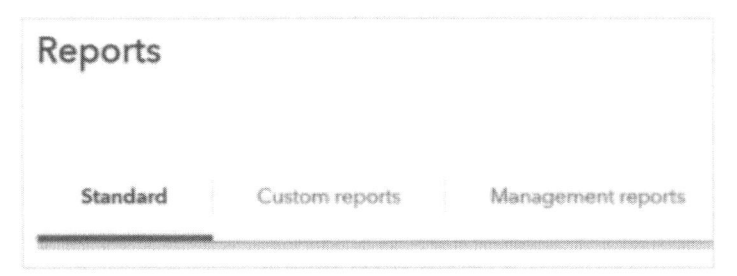

Reports

Standard | Custom reports | Management reports

Standard – this tab includes all the reports included in your subscription. These reports can be customized to fit your needs.

Custom Reports – this tab includes all the reports you have created and saved to have the ability to view them in the future.

Management Reports – this tab includes a professional assembly of the basic management financial statements, typically including a Balance Sheet, Profit & Loss Statement, and Statement of Cash Flows.

From the Reports page, you will find the standard reports are broken down into the following categories:

Favorites – this section is customizable by you. You can select the star next to the reports you commonly use to be included in this listing. A few recommended reports to star (besides the common management reports) would include the Accounts receivable aging detail, Sales by Class Summary, and Deposit Detail.

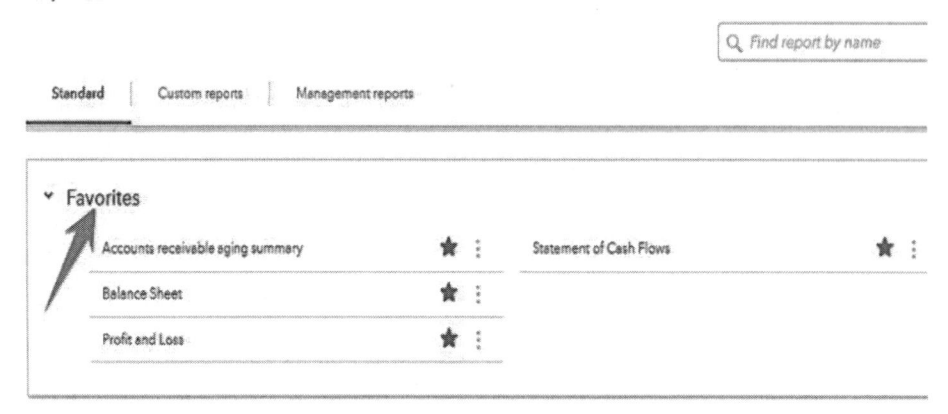

Business overview – includes your key business financials (Balance Sheet & Profit & Loss) in various formats.

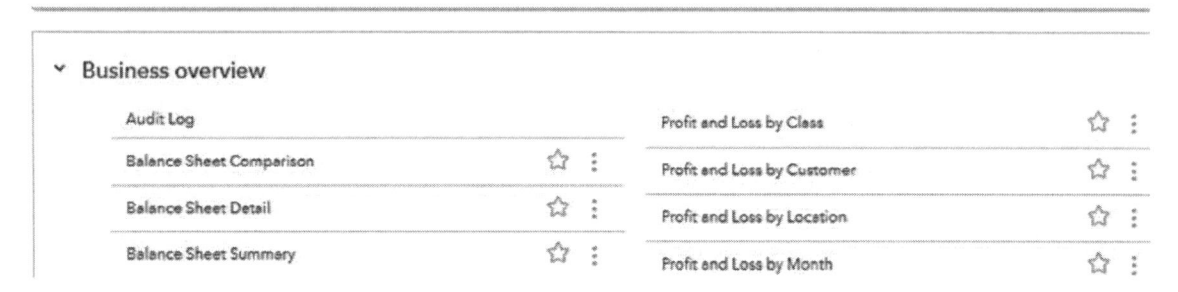

Who owes you – this section includes a variety of reports showing whom you have invoiced, who owes you money, and who has already paid.

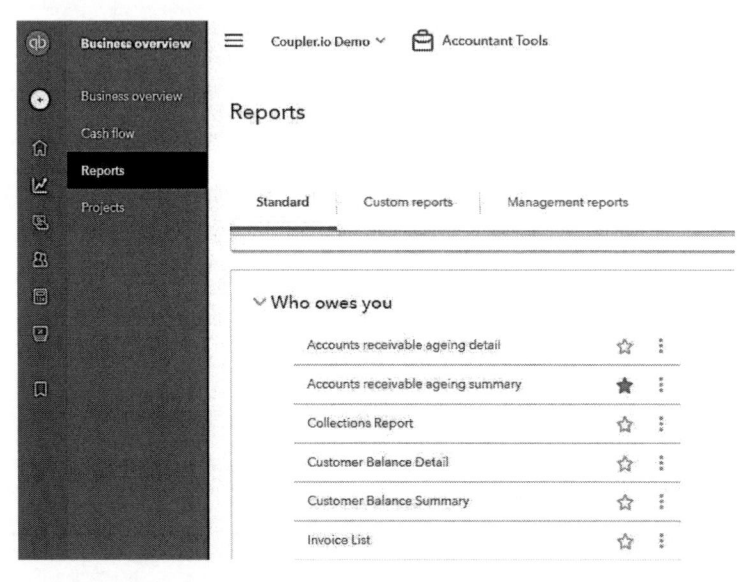

Sales and customers – this section includes all your sales reports and many list reports, including a Customer Contact List and a Product/Service List

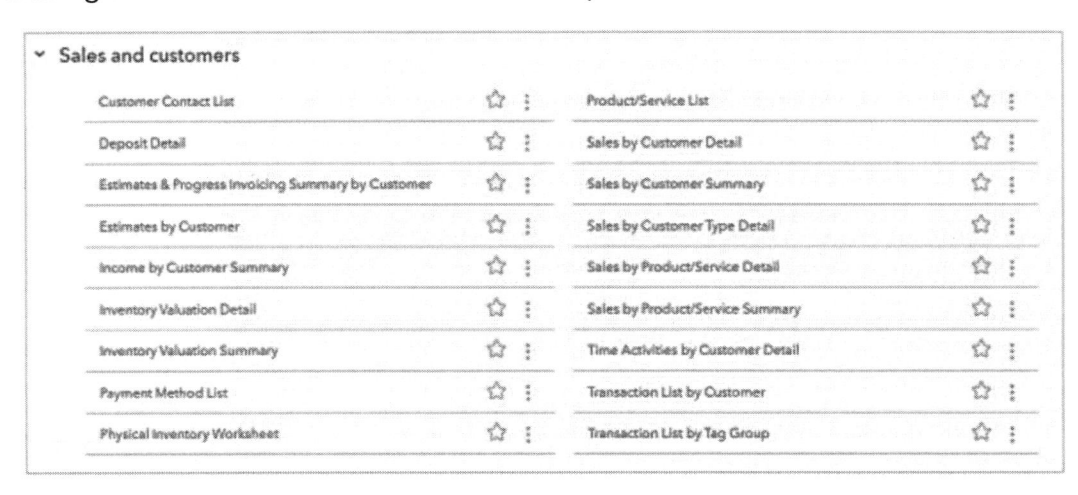

Sales and customers		
Customer Contact List	Product/Service List	
Deposit Detail	Sales by Customer Detail	
Estimates & Progress Invoicing Summary by Customer	Sales by Customer Summary	
Estimates by Customer	Sales by Customer Type Detail	
Income by Customer Summary	Sales by Product/Service Detail	
Inventory Valuation Detail	Sales by Product/Service Summary	
Inventory Valuation Summary	Time Activities by Customer Detail	
Payment Method List	Transaction List by Customer	
Physical Inventory Worksheet	Transaction List by Tag Group	

What you owe – includes payable aging reports and additional reports to track to whom you owe money. Additionally, this section has reports for 1099 contractors.

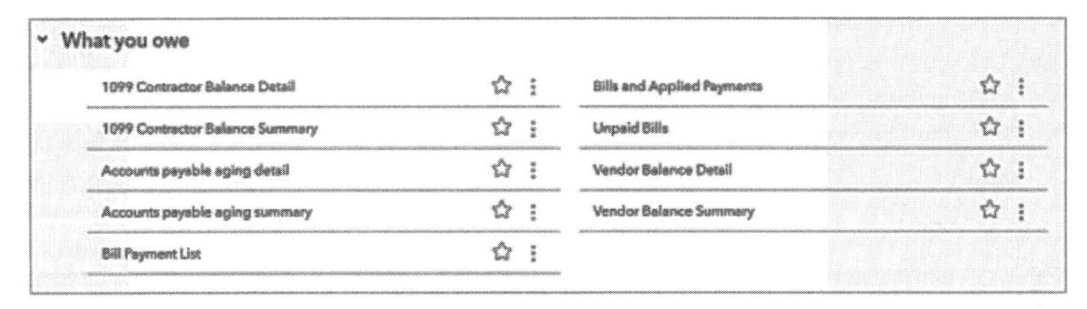

What you owe		
1099 Contractor Balance Detail	Bills and Applied Payments	
1099 Contractor Balance Summary	Unpaid Bills	
Accounts payable aging detail	Vendor Balance Detail	
Accounts payable aging summary	Vendor Balance Summary	
Bill Payment List		

Expenses and vendors – this section includes many reports covering your expenses and vendors. Commonly used reports include the Open Purchase Order List and Transaction List by Vendor.

Expenses and vendors		
1099 Transaction Detail Report	Purchases by Product/Service Detail	
Check Detail	Purchases by Vendor Detail	
Expenses by Vendor Summary	Transaction List by Vendor	
Open Purchase Order List	Vendor Contact List	
Open Purchase Order Detail		

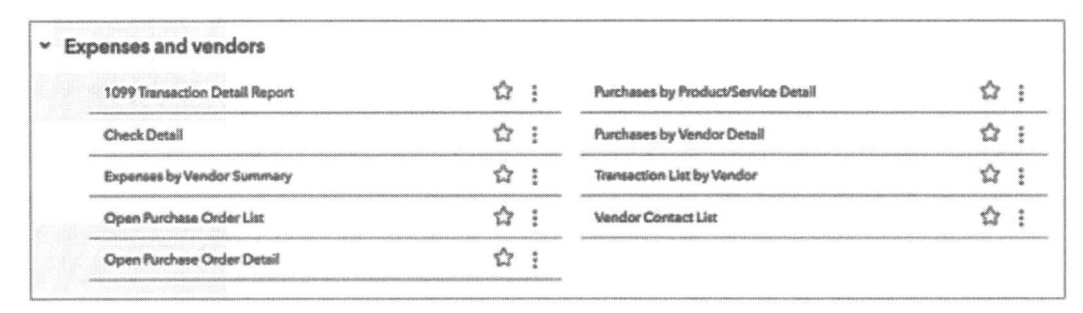

This section includes your sales tax reports that can be used to review your sales tax liability. This section will only be used by companies selling products or services subject to sales tax.

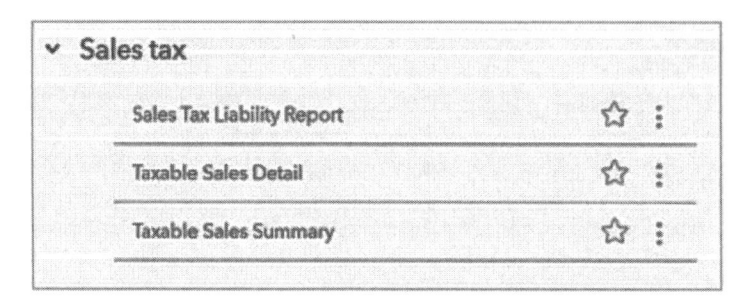

∨ Sales tax	
Sales Tax Liability Report	☆ ⋮
Taxable Sales Detail	☆ ⋮
Taxable Sales Summary	☆ ⋮

Employees – this section provides reports covering your employee time tracking activity.

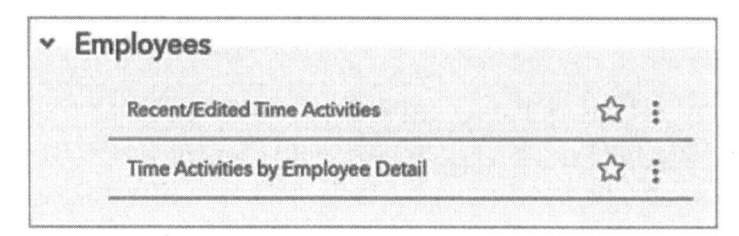

∨ Employees	
Recent/Edited Time Activities	☆ ⋮
Time Activities by Employee Detail	☆ ⋮

For my accountant – this section includes common reports run by accountants. These are not just for your CPA but can be used to understand your business better. Commonly used reports include the Adjusting Journal Entry, General Ledger, and Transaction Detail by Account.

∨ For my accountant			
Account List	☆ ⋮	Recent Transactions	☆ ⋮
Balance Sheet Comparison	☆ ⋮	Reconciliation Reports	☆
Balance Sheet	★ ⋮	Recurring Template List	☆ ⋮
General Ledger	☆ ⋮	Statement of Cash Flows	☆ ⋮
Journal	☆ ⋮	Transaction Detail by Account	☆ ⋮
Profit and Loss Comparison	☆ ⋮	Transaction List by Date	☆ ⋮
Profit and Loss by Tag Group	☆ ⋮	Transaction List with Splits	☆ ⋮
Profit and Loss	★ ⋮	Trial Balance	☆ ⋮
Recent Automatic Transactions	☆ ⋮		

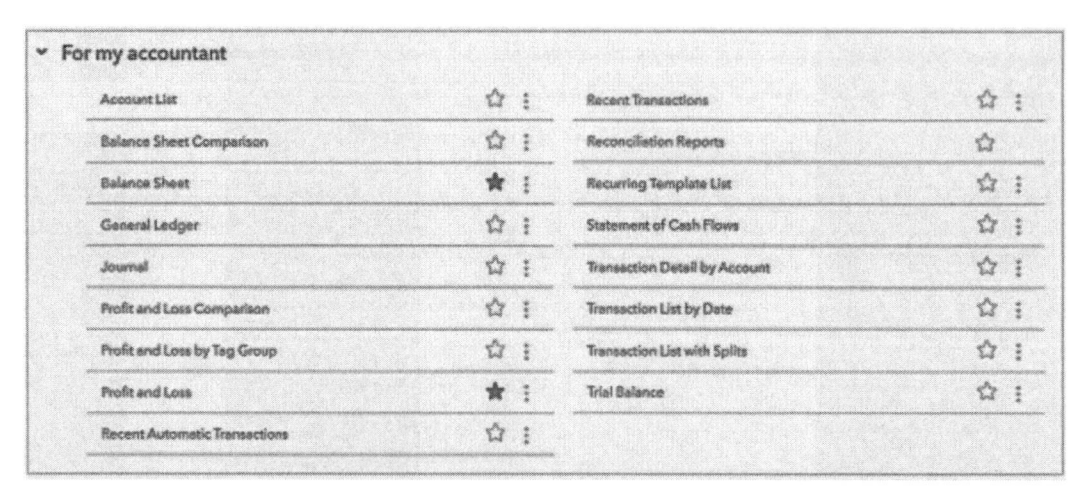

Payroll – this section is for companies running payroll using QuickBooks Online. It includes reports used to review your payroll history, tax liabilities, track employee benefits, and many summary reports.

Payroll			
Employee Details	☆	Payroll Tax Payments	☆
Employee Directory	☆	Payroll Tax and Wage Summary	☆
FFCRA CARES Act Report		Recent/Edited Time Activities	☆
Multiple Worksites	☆	Retirement Plans	☆
Paycheck History	☆	State Mandated Retirement Plans	
Payroll Billing Summary	☆	Time Activities by Employee Detail	☆
Payroll Deductions/Contributions	☆	Total Pay	☆
Payroll Details	☆	Total Payroll Cost	☆
Payroll Summary by Employee	☆	Vacation and Sick Leave	☆
Payroll Summary	☆	Workers' Compensation	☆
Payroll Tax Liability	☆		

Depending on your subscription level (or if you have a payroll), the subscription will dictate the reports you can see and access. All subscriptions will provide the most basic reports, but the higher the subscription level, and the more reports will become available.

QuickBooks Online uses four main types of reports:

Summary Reports

Detail Reports

List Reports

Transaction Reports

Summary Reports

These take all your detailed information and compile them into easy-to-understand reports that can be used to compare data. Summary reports are commonly used because they provide a quick snapshot of your data. Here are some of the most frequently used Summary reports:

1099 Contractor Balance Summary	★	Payroll Billing Summary	★
Accounts payable aging summary	★	Payroll Summary by Employee	★
Accounts receivable aging summary	★	Payroll Summary	★
Balance Sheet Summary	★	Payroll Tax and Wage Summary	★
Customer Balance Summary	★	Quarterly Profit and Loss Summary	★
Estimates & Progress Invoicing Summary by Customer	★	Sales by Customer Summary	★
Expenses by Vendor Summary	★	Sales by Product/Service Summary	★
Income by Customer Summary	★	Taxable Sales Summary	★
Inventory Valuation Summary	★	Vendor Balance Summary	★

Balance Sheet Summary

Profit & Loss Summary

Sales by Class Summary

Accounts Receivable Aging Summary

Accounts Payable Aging Summary

Payroll Summary

Detailed Reports

These provide more information than the summary reports. These are great when you're looking for a specific transaction or want to document your activity in detail. Detailed reports are used primarily to pull detailed information on income, expenses, customers, and suppliers. Here is a list of the most commonly used detailed reports:

1099 Contractor Balance Detail	★	Profit and Loss Detail	★
1099 Transaction Detail Report	★	Purchases by Product/Service Detail	★
Accounts payable aging detail	★	Purchases by Vendor Detail	★
Accounts receivable aging detail	★	Sales by Customer Detail	★
Balance Sheet Detail	★	Sales by Customer Type Detail	★
Check Detail	★	Sales by Product/Service Detail	★
Customer Balance Detail	★	Taxable Sales Detail	★
Deposit Detail	★	Time Activities by Customer Detail	★
Employee Details	★	Time Activities by Employee Detail	★
Inventory Valuation Detail	★	Transaction Detail by Account	★
Open Purchase Order Detail	★	Vendor Balance Detail	★
Payroll Details	★		

Balance Sheet Detail

Profit & Loss Detail

Deposit Detail

Accounts Receivable Aging detail

Customer Balance Detail

Sales by Customer Detail

Accounts Payable Aging Detail

List Reports

These are used to provide detailed information regarding your lists in QuickBooks Online. Lists are used in every aspect of your QuickBooks Online account, including your Chart of Accounts, Customers, Vendors, and Products/Services.

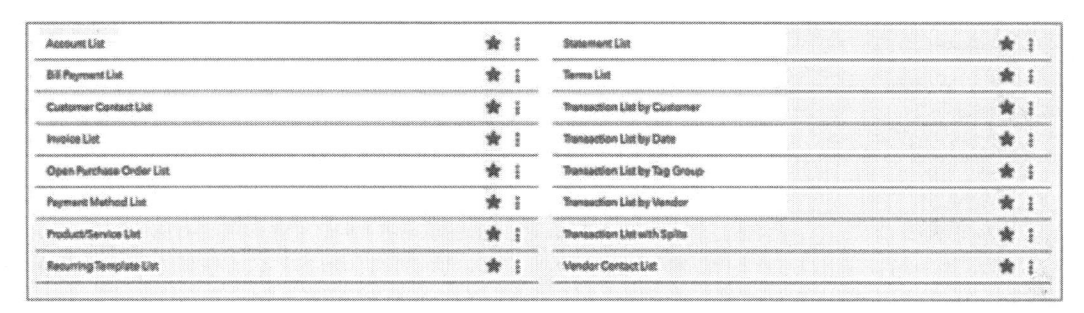

Account List	Statement List
Bill Payment List	Terms List
Customer Contact List	Transaction List by Customer
Invoice List	Transaction List by Date
Open Purchase Order List	Transaction List by Tag Group
Payment Method List	Transaction List by Vendor
Product/Service List	Transaction List with Splits
Recurring Template List	Vendor Contact List

Account List

Class List

Product/Service List

Vendor Contact List

Transaction Reports

These are the most common type of reports generated in QuickBooks Online. They make up most of the reports and provide key data to make better business decisions. Here are some of the most regularly used transaction reports:

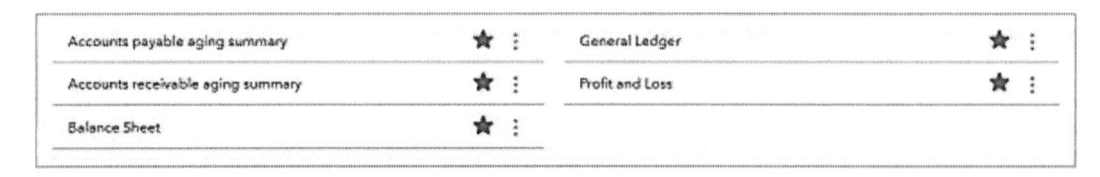

Accounts payable aging summary	★ ⋮	General Ledger	★ ⋮
Accounts receivable aging summary	★ ⋮	Profit and Loss	★ ⋮
Balance Sheet	★ ⋮		

Balance Sheet

Profit & Loss

General Ledger

Accounts Receivable Aging Summary

Accounts Payable Aging Summary

Creating And Saving Customized Reports

Customizing reports allows you to change just about everything in a report, including altering the date range, comparing your data to prior periods, changing accounting methods, and customizing the displayed information. To customize a report, select the report you wish to customize, scroll up and select *Customize.*

The custom options are broken down into the following categories:

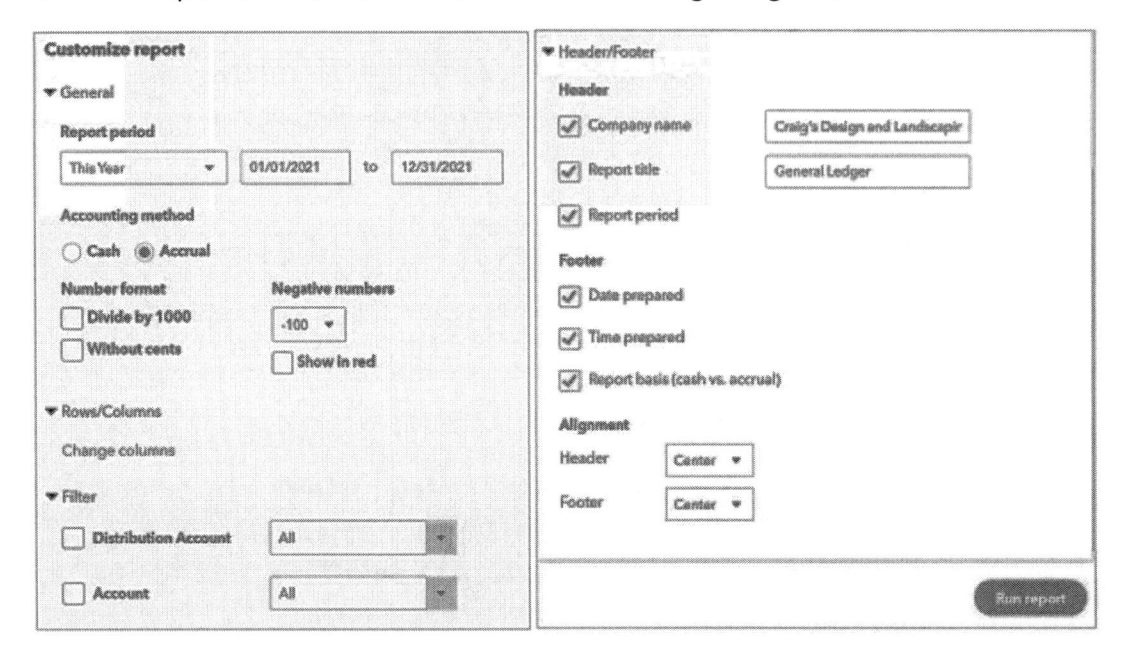

Customize the date range, format, rows, data, and various header and footer options.

General – allows you to select your numbers' reporting period, accounting method, and format.

Rows/Columns – allows you to select the column and comparison column. The comparison column can be either the prior period or the prior year and display the dollar amount or percentage change.

Filter – allows you to select the information you want to be included in your report. You can filter by Customer, Vendor, Class, or Product/Service.

Header/Footer – this allows you to adjust what information is displayed on the header and footer, including the company logo, company name, report title, and report period. The footer includes the date prepared, time prepared, and report basis.

Once you have created the perfect report, it's time to save the report in your "Custom Reports" section. To save a customized report, simply select the green *Save Customization* button. You can rename the report and create groups to categorize your reports. Additionally, you can choose to share your reports with your team or save them for yourself.

Your "Custom Reports" section is easily accessible using the Custom reports tab on the reports home page.

Comparative Reports

Running comparative reports is a great way to evaluate the performance of your business to help make better business decisions. Compare expenses from the prior year, month, week, or another timeframe to determine where your resources are being used. Run comparative reports to evaluate sales growth or trends in your business spending.

Follow these steps to set up and run a comparative report in QuickBooks Online:

From the *Dashboard*, select *Reports*.

Under the "Business Overview" section, select the *Profit and Loss Comparison* report or *Balance Sheet Comparison*.

When viewing the report, scroll up to view the customization options.

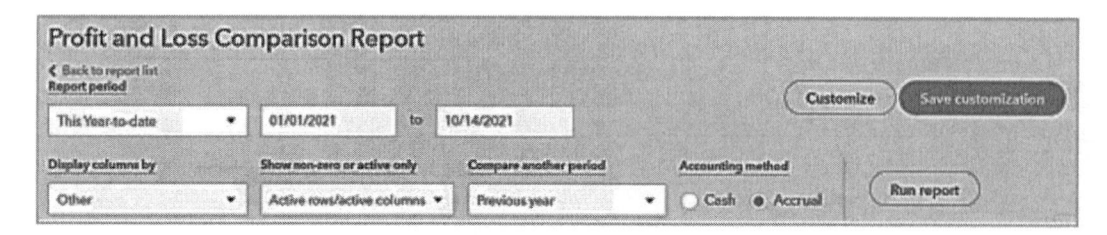

The comparative reports allow you to find variances that may need your attention quickly.

Select the Report Period you wish to display.

Use the drop-down menu under the "Compare another period" section to select the time period you wish to compare the current period against. You can select to view the difference in an additional column and view the change based on a dollar figure or percentage change.

Under the "Accounting Method", select either *Cash or Accrual*.

Select Run Report.

Setting Up Email Schedules For Reports

Instead of running reports at the end of each period, you can have QuickBooks Online email your custom reports automatically. (Keep in mind that this feature is for custom reports only.) This is a great option if you have multiple owners or investors who want periodic reports. Using this option to send third-party institutions' financials (like a bank or lender) is not recommended, as they should be reviewed and approved before sending.

To set up automatic email reports, follow these steps:

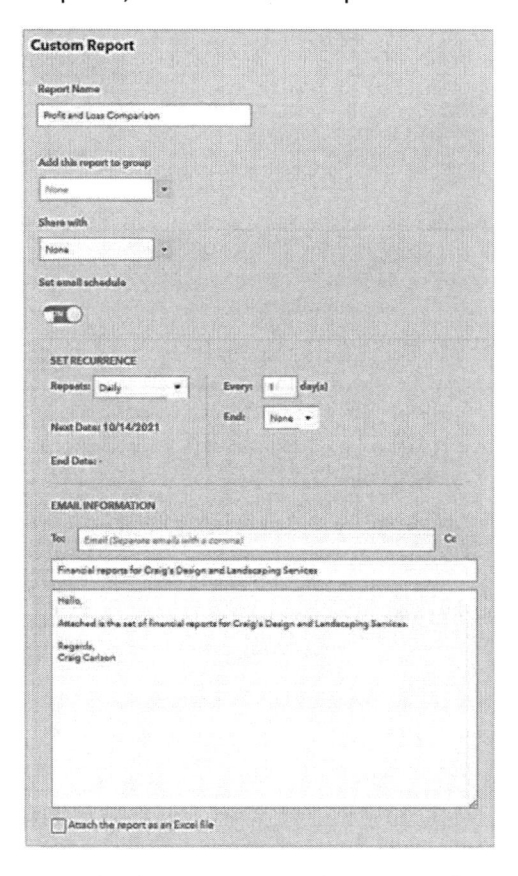

Custom reports allow you to schedule reports to be emailed with a custom message.

From the *Dashboard*, select *Reports* from the left column.

Select the Custom reports tab.

From there, find the report you wish to schedule a reoccurring email.

Select *Edit* ✏ from the "Action" column.

Under "Set email schedule", use the toggle to select *ON*.

Select the recurrence schedule (how often the reports are emailed).

Enter the recipient's email address(es).

Edit the email subject title and body of the email.

Once you are happy with your selections, select *Save and close*.

Audit Log

One of the largest advantages of QuickBooks Online is that it's easily accessible by your employees and accountants. With multiple people in your books, it's important to record what adjustments were made and who made them. The audit log does just that and tracks all the changes in your books and who made each adjustment.

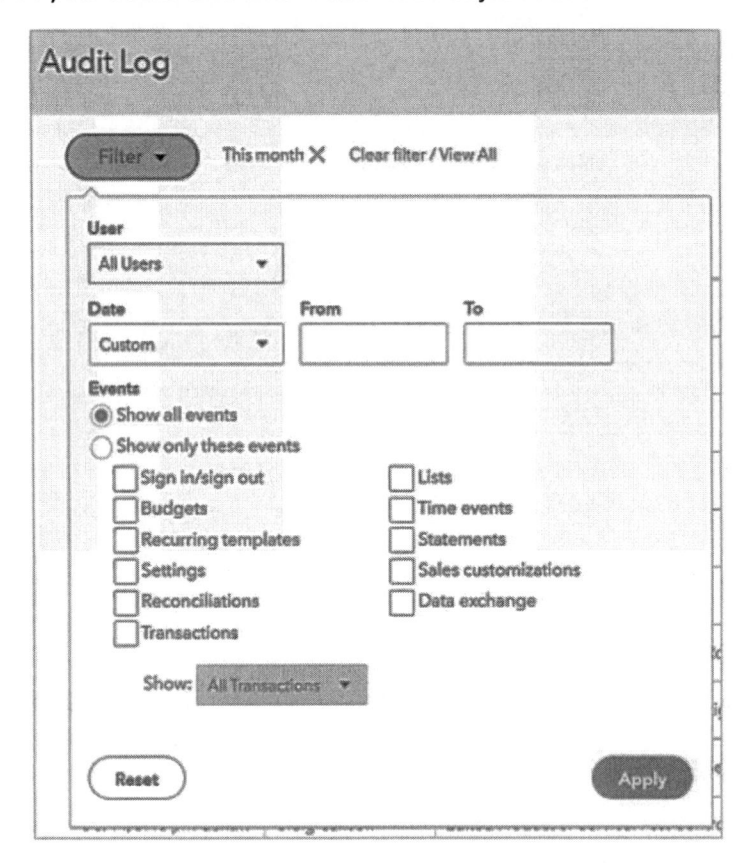

The audit log filter allows you to select the user or date range to narrow your search—track who made adjustments to your books and when.

From the *Dashboard*, select the *Settings* icon (⚙).

Select *Audit Log* from the "Tools" column.

Select the *Filter* to select the user, date, and type of transaction.

Select *Apply*.

The Audit log will list all the transactions starting with the most recent. Select the event or history to view more information on a specific transaction.

Conclusion

Every SME business, as I already stated, has a need, and this need is dependent on what the business wants to achieve. If these needs are not met, it might not be easy to achieve the goals of this business. One of the principal needs of every business is the need to manage all the accounting details properly. It will help the company grow monetarily, and this growth will ensure the continued sustenance of these businesses. The primary issue is that most companies do not begin with knowledgeable people in the accounting field.

QuickBooks Online changes how you manage your accounting by giving you an innovative and user-friendly application. The software was designed with beginners in mind but can be adopted by more experienced users.

This platform is loaded with reporting, invoicing, and analytical tools to help maintain a business's cash flow.

Besides monetary matters, QuickBooks Online also helps track employee hours and automobile mileage. Your drivers can use the mobile app to track their routes so you know where your vehicles are at all times.

Automating custom reports, generating invoices, and sorting documents are easier than ever. The best thing about it is that your data is secured on Intuit's 128-bit encrypted server, safe from malicious internet attacks.

The need for having small and medium enterprise (SME) business owners manage the accounting aspect of their businesses to meet their needs is the drive behind the development of QuickBooks Online.

It means that even if you are not knowledgeable in the intricacies of accounting, you can still correctly manage the accounting and monetary aspect of your business based on what your business needs using QuickBooks Online.

QuickBooks Online has many more features than what we have here, but this is an excellent place to begin if you are a beginner. With the details provided here, you should navigate successfully through this software and use it to carry out all the accounting functions you need for the proper management of your business. With the knowledge in this book and your active implementations of the steps for maximizing every function in this software, you will have nothing short of a smooth sale in managing the accounting aspect of your business to meet your needs.

Glossary

A

Accountant: Determining how an enterprise is performing financially, keeping track of company transactions, and providing financial statements is the primary job of an accountant. With knowledge of finance, math, and law these individuals provide investors and organization owners with thorough details about business performance.

Accounting: Accounting is the activity of analyzing one's business's financial records. Daily fiscal information is unraveled into straightforward data, so companies can understand their cash flow better. Organization owners can measure the health of their enterprise with outcomes reported by regulatory authorities, creditors, investors, and others.

Accounting Cycle: A particular period can be tracked through the accounting cycle's progress. Each deal is monitored from the time it happens until the company's finances are affected.

Accounting Period: The period in which a group of financial statements are segmented is what's known as an accounting period. Investors and company owners utilize this process to look at the contrast between months or a year.

Account Payable: Debts to third parties are tracked with Account payable. Liabilities and other monetary obligations from suppliers or vendors are recorded with this task. Things like the internet, telephone, and electricity can become part of this expense list. It is vital to use an account payable to direct your company's cash flow.

Account Receivable: The debt that a customer owes to an enterprise is what is called an account receivable. Generally, a company informs the client how much they owe by sending an invoice. Accounts receivable are included on a balance sheet because it's cash the consumer is expected to pay.

Accrual Accounting: This form of accounting allows deals to be displayed when they occur. Typically, accrual accounting is used for medium to large organizations. If a company is not paid instantly after submitting an invoice, this kind of bookkeeping can help keep things on track.

Accrual Basis Accounting: Income recorded upon receipt and costs declared as soon as they occur are the foundation for the accrual accounting method. This is the most accurate way to track old inventory, sales allowances, and product returns.

Accruals: Payment for sales or invoices that have not occurred is recorded with accruals. There are also expense accruals, including tax obligations, receivable accounts, and interest earned.

Accrued Expenses: These expenses have not been paid yet, but have been recorded. Spontaneous liabilities or accrued liabilities are what some refer to as accrued expenses. Think of a major repair in the last month of the fiscal year, which is only paid upon receiving the bill.

Accrual Method Accounting: The year in which your income is earned is the basis for the accrual method of accounting. This gives company owners a better overall view of how their business performed financially over a specific yearly period.

Amortization: This strategy is implemented by business owners to reduce the expense of an intangible asset or loan over a certain period of time. It can extend the loan period so that there is less pressure on the company.

Assets: Anything that is a business resource or contains value is known as an asset. Depending on the scenario, an asset can benefit the company when it uses it. Within a year, non-fixed assets can be converted to their equivalent in monetary value. Examples of intangible items include trademarks, patents, copyrights, and shares. Inventory, materials, property, furniture, and money are considered tangible assets.

Audit: Ensuring accurate and fair records are kept is crucial for any business. Financial audits can be performed by an external accounting firm or from within the enterprise. At the end of the fiscal year, most businesses do a thorough audit so they can determine profitability.

B

Bad Debt Expense: When a client can't afford a business product or service, a bad debt expense is documented. Most companies tend to work with credit to gain more customers or to make their lives easier. Here is an example: If a consumer has 20 days to pay and doesn't, you can record it as a bad debt expense. Utilize the write-off technique to change accounts receivable and bad debt expenditure.

Bad Debt: Outstanding client balances can be documented as a company's bad debt. This is only if the owner believes that the money won't be paid in the future or if there is evidence that the client can't pay it back.

Balance Sheet: The financial health of a business is determined by a balance sheet. Accessing how cash is exiting and entering a company allows owners to take full advantage of optimization. Balance sheets are generated annually, quarterly, and monthly.

Balloon Payment: A lump sum payment and a balloon payment are the same thing. It is when a client or a business decides to make a one-time payment to settle outstanding debt. A balloon payment agreement also lets the individual receive a discount on the amount owed.

Bookkeeping: Maintaining succinct transaction records and recording a business' deals is called bookkeeping. Once bookkeepers have gathered all the relevant information, they can relay in-depth reports to business owners.

Bootstrapping: Beginning a company with minimal cash is tough for company proprietors. Bootstrapping means that a person starts their own business with their own cash.

C

Capital: The money used to run an organization is capital. Liquid assets or cash that help make business purchases are vital to a company's success. Trading capital, equity, debt, and working capital are the key monetary holdings of an enterprise.

Capital Cost: When a company takes on debt, uses collateral, or spends cash to add value while purchasing new assets, it equates to a capital cost. Single-time payments are capital costs as long as they're put toward services and products that benefit the organization.

Cash: Cash is money, and money makes the world go round. Without the liquidity of legal tender, businesses would be unable to keep up with day-to-day expenses. At the top of a balance sheet appears a company's cash balance.

Cash Accounting: Records of transactions received are the process of cash accounting. When payment is made, the cost is recorded immediately. This provides a comprehensible view of an organization constantly.

Cash Basis Accounting: Start-ups and small businesses love using cash basis accounting because it is efficient. After payments are given or received, it's vital to record them as either expenditure or revenue. A downfall of these methods is that they exaggerate the robustness of a business.

Cash Equivalents: Short-term assets are considered to be highly liquid and can be converted into money, generally within three months. Putting cash into interest-earning investment institutes, such as commercial paper, treasury bills, bonds, and stocks, is a good way to increase an organization's health.

Cash Flow: The amount of money that flows in and out of a business is what accountants call cash flow. Without cash flow, an enterprise may struggle to stay afloat and maintain its regular expenses.

Cash Flow Statement: A cash flow statement is a report of the money that goes in and out of a business. Any legal tender earned or spent is displayed as pecuniary sources on these documents.

Cash Method Accounting: If you want to view expenses and income, utilizing cash method accounting is the best solution. Receivable and payable accounts won't appear as pending deals if your company uses this accounting technique.

Cash on Hand: Any money that hasn't been placed into the bank, such as legal tender from a business's register, is cash on hand.

CGT - Capital Gain Tax: Once an investment or asset is sold, you will pay tax for its earnings. Tax implications are applied depending on if the capital gain tax is long-term or short-term.

Chart of Accounts: All financial accounts are shown within a business's chart of accounts. Company owners can see daily expenses associated with maintaining the enterprise. Subcategories make it easy to separate costs, revenue, equity, liabilities, and assets for an intricate analysis.

Cost of Goods Sold: The cost of sale and the cost of goods sold are identical. These expenses involve the purchase or manufacturing of an item a business sells. All values, including shipping, overheads, labor expenses, and raw materials, are categorized under the cost of goods sold.

Credit: Credit can be explained in two ways. When a company supplies services or products to another party via debenture, there is a correlation. The first party will set out an agreement that the other entities will pay for services rendered at a later date. However, credit can also be utilized to report how a company has received the money. Credits are deposits that come into an organization and can be viewed on the right-hand side of the account register.

Credit Entries: An accounting journal holds multiple records, and credit entries are one of them. Understanding the importance of this entry can help company owners keep precise records. Whether cash is received or given credit, entries help to maintain the balance of an enterprise's books.

Crowdfunding: Indiegogo, GoFundMe, and Kickstarter are crowdfunding websites. This financial backing method allows new business owners to ask others to invest as much or little. Both parties can benefit tremendously from using crowdfunding. Ensure you look at the advantages and disadvantages before signing up with one of these platforms.

Current Assets: Assets that can be utilized within one year, consumed, or sold are classified as current. Business balance sheets reflect this information and allow proprietors to know what is happening daily within their organization. Current assets include liquid assets, inventory, accounts receivable, prepaid expenses, investments, cash equivalents, and foreign legal tenders.

Current Liabilities: Anything that must be paid within a traditional company operation cycle or a year is current liabilities. Money that's owed, such as outstanding debts, deferred revenue, dividends payable, income taxes owed, or payroll, is included. Using the current assets available, business owners can pay these expenses.

D

Debit: When a business pays a supplier or vendor, this is recorded as a debit. On a ledger account, this data is found on the left-hand side. Debits occur when liabilities or assets decrease or increase and correlate with financial obligations, lowering of income, purchasing additional assets, and other expenses.

Debit Entries: Much like credit entries, these records are reported in a company's accounting journal. However, debit entries operate the opposite to the latter by increasing an expense or asset account.

Debt: Money owed by a person or company is considered debt. Generally, debt contains interest and is borrowed by enterprises to cover expenses they can't afford during a particular period. There is good and bad debt, so understand both before taking out a loan.

Depreciation: When equipment or assets in a company lose their value, they are considered depreciated. The expected lifespan of these items is the primary factor helping to calculate depreciation. Assets like machinery, automobiles, printers, computers, and other tangible items all lose monetary value. Without affecting a company's profit, depreciation allows owners to document expenses through accretion instead of a once-off cost.

Double Entry Bookkeeping: Every story has two sides, and so does double entry bookkeeping. A formula exists on balance sheets that calculates assets, liabilities, and equity to maintain a business's accountancy correctness. Double-entry bookkeeping works because its assets equal liabilities and equity.

E

Encumbered Assets: If a third-party business has a legal claim to an asset that another company owns, then it's an encumbered asset. An example is when a company owns stocks and wants to lend money to purchase new appliances or computers, these investments become an encumbered asset. If the business cannot pay the money back the creditors may utilize the stocks to cover the pending expense.

EOFY: The end of a fiscal or financial year is a stressful time for all. For one year of commerce, a business requires reporting the EOFY for tax purposes. Depending on the state the company owner lives in, their financial year ends at a different time.

Equity: Equity has two meanings: Either the potential value of a company or the amount of cash that shareholders or the proprietor have invested in the organization. A business's net worth is essentially calculated by determining its equity.

F

FBT: Fringe benefits tax is payment made to staff over and above their typical wage or salary. These advantages can be paid to the associates or family members of the employee but at the employer's discretion. FBT can include paying for rent, meals or drinks, gym memberships, work vehicles, and more.

Financial Statements: A company's activities and monetary obligations are displayed on financial statements. Accountants require these reports to prepare a business for auditing, tax returns, and investigation by government agencies. Cash flow statements, income statements, and balance sheets are the foundation of financial statements.

Financial Year: The 12 months a business operates within is a "financial year." It's a federal regulation that all companies must conclude the year with a financial statement. Organization owners can also use this financial year report to measure loss, profit, or budget.

Fiscal Year: Preparing and providing financial statements is required each fiscal year. The company selects the date it wishes to report economic data to the government. Based on the nature of their dealings, organizations, enterprises, and countries can dictate when this period begins and ends.

Fixed Assets: These assets are bought by a company and are not converted to money easily. Non-current or long-term assets are also considered fixed assets. These items are purchased to be transformed into cash after one year or are expected to last much longer. That means a company can use depreciation to lower the product's value because of the wear and tear associations attached to it.

Fixed Expense: A fixed expense is a cost a business incurs that is identical each time it is paid. Annually, quarterly, monthly, or weekly are the most common ways that business owners cover these expenses. However, these rates can change even though they are fixed. Expenses such as rent, car payments, employee wages, and real estate tax may be adjusted during the renewal stage.

Forecasting: Financial forecasting allows companies to determine potential income in the future. It takes past and present financial data to establish the figures required to make this prediction. Use forecasting to dictate how cash flow and annual budgets are stipulated.

G

General Ledger: General ledgers help company owners manage all their organization's monetary transactions in a single location. All a business's financial accounts are shown within a general ledger, such as losses, profits, and balance sheets. These ledgers are the rudimentary aspects of an organization.

Goodwill: When a company buys another company, goodwill is included. The figure paid for the organization minus the intangible assets, tangible assets, and debts is benevolence. Balance sheets display goodwill only at the time of the sale of the business. An example is if a company sells for $700,000, its assets equate to $300,000, and liabilities are $50,000. The remaining $350,000 is considered goodwill and may be based on numerous factors, including employee relations, reputable customers, exceptional social media following, solid client base, and quality branding.

Gross Profit: After deducting costs affiliated with distributing and producing services or products, a business is left with its gross profit. Gross profits equal total sales minus the cost of goods sold.

Gross Profit Margin: An organization's gross earnings are determined by the gross profit margin. Once owners have covered expenses such as directly associated costs, materials, and labor, they're left with a figure. Generally, the gross profit margin is shown as a percentage, making overall business analysis easier. Calculate the amount by dividing net sales by the cost of goods sold or direct expenses.

I

Income: Any money that comes into a company by selling services or products is considered income. If a print shop charges $1 per print and sells 20 prints, its income is $20. Government institutes use the income to determine how much tax a business must pay. These regulatory bodies deducted expenses from income to come up with a figure that was reasonable and acceptable to the company owner.

Income Statement: An income statement displays whether an organization has lost or gained cash over a specific period. The creditworthiness of a business is determined by banks using an income statement. These reports are one of the three crucial statements, the other two being a balance sheet and a cash flow statement.

Income Tax: Governments apply income tax to people or businesses performing operations within specific jurisdictions. A progressive tax system is employed by most countries and charges relevant tax based on earnings.

Insolvency: Being unable to pay one's debts is insolvency. Cash flow and balance sheet insolvency are the two types of bankruptcy that can be filed. If a business cannot pay its debts but has adequate assets, it's called cash flow insolvency. Balance sheet insolvency is when an organization doesn't have the liquidity to pay its loans.

Intangible Assets: Trademarks, patents, and license agreements are intangible assets. These assets are not readily identifiable and do not exist in a physical form.

Inventory: Stock and inventory are the same thing. The material used in producing products or services is a company's inventory. Works in progress, finished commodities, and raw materials are the three main categories these items are placed in.

Invoice: Invoices are legal records of an exchange of services or goods. It reflects the costs connected to the purchase and typically includes both client and business credentials. The deadline for payment is often attached to these bills.

J

Journal: Traditional and high-volume transactions are kept within a company's accounting journal. There are a variety of journals, including general, purchasing, and sales. Once recorded in the book, transactional information is then recorded in the general ledger.

L

Liabilities: Any debt a business has is considered a liability. Previous company transactions that benefit the business long-term, such as the exchange of services or products and sales of assets fall in this category. Short-term liabilities, like a credit card, can also affect your organization yearly.

Liability Account: Legally binding debts owed to an entity are recorded in a liability account. These figures are included in a business's balance sheet and general ledger. Money owed to vendors or suppliers who provided it on credit is documented with this accounting feature.

Liquidate: When a business's finances are unbalanced, it may need to liquidate to cover debts. A company will sell its assets and use the proceeds to pay off money owed. During the process, any items not sold to pay off shareholders or lenders retain ownership of the proprietor.

Liquidity: The ease of turning an asset into money is liquidity. Without affecting the price of an item when it is bought and sold, liquidity shows a business can cover short-term liabilities. Ratios or percentages provide an overall view of an organization's financial health.

Long-Term Liabilities: If a company owes money to another entity over an extended period, it's a long-term liability. Generally, these debts exceed the 12-month range and sometimes even further. These debts are separate from the remaining expenses the company owes.

M

Margin: Minus expense from revenue, and a business is left with its margin. This figure displays how efficient an organization is.

Marketable Securities: Turning assets into money quickly is considered a form of marketable security. Companies can buy and sell these assets effortlessly, receive a lower return rate than other securities, or transfer them to a stock exchange.

N

Net: After deductions are removed, the figure remaining is a company's net. Net income or earnings are what remains once all costs are subtracted. These expenses include returns, net revenue, and liability deductions.

Net Income: Net income remains after the organization's expenses are removed from its proceeds. Some deductions can also include additional sources of income, such as the purchase of stocks, shares, or other investments.

Net Profit: Take the total earnings of a business minus expenses; the net profit is the remaining figure. A financial statement may list a company's net profit as "net profit after taxes."

Non-Current Assets: Assets held by a company for more than one year are non-current assets. An organization uses these items to generate income over an extended period. Generally, these assets have exponential value and cannot be exchanged for cash quickly.

Non-Current Liabilities: Non-current liabilities are financial obligations or debts that don't need to be paid within a year. Bonds, long-term leases, and credit are some of the non-current liabilities in this category.

Non-Operating Assets: If a business makes no money from an item, it's a non-operating asset. Idle equipment, outdated machinery, land not being utilized, and vacant buildings fall under this classification.

O

Operating Assets: Running a company's daily operations requires operating assets. Anything that helps the organization make cash is considered vital, no matter how stable the financial health of a business is. These assets are needed to run the company and are not for sale.

Operational Expense: Operating expenses and operational expenses are the same. These costs are the expenses that help a business function but do not include the charges for delivering or creating a service or product. Advertising, automobiles, computers, and even printer paper are what a company can consider an operational expense.

Overheads: The daily expenses incurred by an organization is its overheads. Specific business activities or costs are traced but do not affect the foundation of a company. Internet, gas, utility bills, legal fees, salaries, and a secretary all fall under this category.

Owner's Equity: The amount a proprietor has invested in their company, minus the figure they have taken out, is the owner's equity. Once all liabilities are removed, the remaining cash belongs to the business holder.

P

Payroll: Salaries or wages are recorded on a business's payroll. It helps the owner monitor taxes and payments throughout the year. The total money spent on workers or the number of staff who work for the company can be referred to as payroll.

Payslip: A payslip is a document an individual receives once they have been paid by a company. It helps keep records for the owner and worker alike.

Petty Cash: A limited amount of legal tender available to businesses for daily company operations is petty cash. It can be a few hundred dollars or $30 and can be used for small purchases that don't require a check or credit facility.

Prepaid Expenses: Costs recorded later after payments have been made are prepaid expenses. On the balance sheet, these charges are documented as assets because of forthcoming financial benefits. When the advantages are achieved, the figure is registered as an expense.

Profit: Minus cash earned from money spent, and you're left with a profit. Consistent profitability also demonstrates that an enterprise has adequate financial health. Reinvesting cash into a company is the best way to help it grow exponentially.

Profit and Loss: Revenue minus expense equals the profit and loss of an organization. The money received and the cash spent are other definitions of this figure.

Profit and Loss Statement: A report providing the owners with business profits, losses, expenses, and sales is a profit and loss statement. Determining a company's accomplishments via a monthly, quarterly, or annual evaluation with this report is recommended.

R

Receipt: Whether it's an electronic record or a piece of paper, this document indicates a business has collected cash from a buyer.

Retained Earnings: The amount of money retained for reinvestment in the business is retained earnings. Money of this nature can be kept for various reasons, including paying off debt, fixing asset purchases, and working capital.

Revenue: The total cash made by a business from selling its services or products is the revenue.

ROI: The return on investment formula helps a business's investors determine how a company performs compared to others. The amount lost or made on the investment is what ROI provides and is typically calculated as a percentage.

S

Statement of Cash Flow: The balance sheet and income statement are interconnected in these statements. It shows the outflow and inflow of cash into a business. It's a fundamental aspect of any company. It's also referred to as a cash flow report.

Stock: Inventory and stock are the same. These items range from raw materials, components, or products an enterprise utilizes daily.

Stock Taking: Stock taking involves counting inventory to confirm a company's book balance with its held items.

T

Tangible Assets: Assets with a physical form are tangible. These items are crucial to a business and hold real value. Fixed and current are the two types of tangible assets that exist. Machinery, equipment, and items that last for multiple years are considered fixed. Current assets include stocks, futures, or bonds.

Trial Balance: If a business owner needs to view the balance of their general ledger, they can use a trial balance to achieve it. This process can be performed at any time and may include a specific date range.

V

Variable Expense: These costs change depending on the type of service or product utilized. It is possible that variable expenses can differ from month to month. Ensure adequate provisions are made for these fees, as they can be challenging to manage over the long term.

W

Working Capital: Current liabilities minus current assets equals a business's working capital.

Write Off: When the value of an asset is recorded and deleted from the financial records, it's a write-off. Once this occurs, all monetary value is removed from the item, no matter what.

Printed in Great Britain
by Amazon